MIND FOOD

MIND FOOD

PLANT-BASED RECIPES FOR POSITIVE MENTAL HEALTH

LAUREN LOVATT

Photography by
Sara Kiyo Popowa
@shisodelicious

Leaping Hare Press

CONTENTS

DRINKS
108

DESSERTS
120

PANTRY STAPLES
146

FAR OUT FERMENTATION
160

MAKE A BATCH
170

INTRODUCTION

MENTAL HEALTH HAS AFFECTED ME in many ways over the years. I have watched close friends suffer and fail to manage illnesses, noticed mental health go uncared for, witnessed first-hand the stigma and seen the personal struggles of people desperately trying to get help yet getting nowhere within an impersonal system.

I have experienced mental health issues myself and fallen through the gaps when trying to reach out for help. Without good support, perseverance and a great deal of luck, I wouldn't be here today. These experiences have led me to think about what I needed when I was at an all-time low. Following my own mental health struggles, I have noticed not only what we need to do to overcome and manage a variety of illnesses but how we can support our mental health day to day and pondered why a healthy mind is not more widely accepted as the most important part of everyone's overall wellbeing.

My route to recovery from mental illness has led me to realize what I need to do to feed my mind and, through a lengthy process of trial and error, I have been able to put basic lifestyle and nutrition knowledge into practice and understand what works best for me. After I became a professional chef, teacher and food designer, I gained a good understanding of ways to make this Mind Food life the most delicious it can possibly be and this book is my way of sharing this knowledge with you.

Mind Food embodies a lifestyle focused on prevention rather than cure. This book is not just about making recovery from mental illness more accessible to those suffering, but also about promoting lifestyle values that can lead anyone to better support their own brains through the way they choose to live.

Often, we just don't know where to turn for guidance when we do experience issues with our mental health. We may not know the options or routes to recovery and we can be unsure how to help ourselves through lifestyle actions. Issues like anxiety, depression, OCD and even bipolar disorder or Alzheimer's can be supported with good nutrition, in some cases alongside medication.

Food for the mind needs to be common knowledge and I hope within this book you see easy, delicious and practical ways to feed your mind every day.

WHAT IS MIND FOOD?

Our brain not only impacts how we feel every day but how we sleep, work, move and thrive. It is important to care for it now, as the choices we make every day affect much more than we often realize and can be carried into our old age. Right now, terms like mental fitness, brain care and mental wellbeing are all becoming more commonplace, and there are brands emerging that embrace brain care as a category. As we discover and learn about this fundamental part of our health and life it seems practical actions are still not widely understood.

Nutrition is the single most important factor in our mental health. The reality is that most of us don't get what we need from our day-to-day diet, which is something we delve deep into in this book, sharing actionable recipes and ideas for you to incorporate into your life. Eating the right foods can help change everything, and as diet is ever more widely researched it has been proven repeatedly to support and resolve a wide variety of issues. The *Mind Food* menu takes inspiration from my own food experiences to brighten up your plate with foods that are plant-rich, filled with fibre and whole grains, prioritizing nutrient-dense foods with vibrant colours, mixed with good-quality proteins, healthy fats and omega-3s. Mind Food is rich in antioxidants and anti-inflammatory ingredients and embraces the power of tonic herbs and medicinal plants to relieve stress and support brain function.

Mental health is defined by the World Health Organization (WHO) as 'a state of wellbeing in which every individual realizes their own potential, can cope with the normal stress of life, can be productive and contribute to the community'.

Mind Food is not just about the ingredients we serve, but about the act of coming together around food, using food and cooking as a form of connection and self-expression to take our mind to a different place away from immediate concerns. It is about everyday rituals, useful ideas, ingredient knowledge and easy practices that can help us all to make this way of living more accessible.

Our mental health is also affected by lifestyle factors other than food, such as sleep, connection to others, exercise, mindfulness, hydration and how and where we spend our days. The most crucial steps we can take to change mental health globally are to raise awareness of what a Mind Food lifestyle is, better understand and implement the lifestyle factors that affect our mental health, talk more openly about the potential symptoms of poor mental health, share the wide variety of more personalized therapies and create more concepts, ideas and resources for people of all ages to learn from and understand. This will help us all to better support ourselves in making prevention rather than cure the priority.

HOW CAN MIND FOOD HELP?

I have written this book to help you reimagine the way you think about mental health in parallel with food. At this moment there are still so many misconceptions, assumptions and stigmas on many levels. Having lived the Mind Food life first-hand, I'm sharing my story and experiences in these pages to inspire others to share theirs and to show we are all on a spectrum of mental health and this will constantly fluctuate but there is always a way to better support it ourselves.

Mind Food explores a tangible lifestyle framework for mental health using seasonal, whole ingredients with sprinkles of tonic herbs to create the most delicious and nutritious Mind Food meals. This book provides a toolbox of ingredients, recipes and ideas that I hope you will pick up at different points in your life, which you can customize each and every day and which will be useful and empowering to adapt into your own routine.

Know that you can do anything you set your mind to, even though there will always be those who try and hold you back, aren't ready to see your transformation and even just don't get it. Remember that's just where they are in their journey and continue to move forward with yours.

I hope to give you the ability to build your confidence with food filled with tasty ingredients that make you feel good inside and out. On page 13 of this book, you will see a key to guide you when you are searching for a certain feeling. You can enjoy any recipe at any time, but at the top of each recipe there is a 'mood', explained in the guide, to show how the recipe can make you feel. If used in a personalized way, I hope these ideas open up a new way of thinking about food that goes far beyond just flavour and nutrition, to have the power to transform the way we think, feel and see the world.

MY MIND FOOD STORY

Trigger warning: suicide and eating disorder references below

I've always loved food. My earliest memories include getting covered in berries when picking them from the bush as a child, devouring home-cooked roast dinners and being extremely experimental trying all sorts of delicacies on holidays around the world. I would derive such pleasure from cooking decadent meals for my family, mastering soufflés, poring through recipe books, spending hours inventing mystery sauces and doing everything possible to experience new flavours and ideas I could share with those around me. Food has always made me happy, it is my way of connecting with people, sharing delicious experiences and expressing myself.

Food never seemed like an option as a career, so I went to university to study Art. I continued cooking, making comforting bowls of dauphinoise potatoes after nights out, cooking with friends and spending time making my favourite recipes. Very early on I met someone who lit up every room, shared ideas I had never heard of and looked at me in a way I had never experienced before. Rishi was a photographer, funny, creative, confident, and we very quickly became a couple.

During this time, I started to notice that Rishi's down days were lower than low and when things were good, they were out of control. Until this time, I hadn't really thought about mental health, good or bad, but early on in our relationship it was clear something was not ok. After months of reaching out for support through counselling, Rishi was diagnosed with bipolar disorder. This lead to a difficult time trying to support him, and we discovered that there was nowhere within the health system to turn for help as the waiting lists were too long and everyone around him felt helpless. To see someone suffer so much with something 'invisible' was devastating, that feeling of total hopelessness was tough especially when that person suffering so much behind closed doors was the one offering so much light and support to others and had talent and passion bursting from the seams. After a long train of events, ups, downs, fights, adventures and months of being pushed away, I woke up one morning to a phone call from Rishi's twin brother, saying that Rishi had taken his own life. This was a devastating shock for everyone who knew him and for me, my world turned upside down.

I remember a year of feeling in total limbo and not knowing how to process this terrible turn of events, so after a year of crying and confusion, my focus shifted into obsession and my passion for food became a distraction from the pain. I unconsciously became all-consumed by a concoction of eating disorders and depression, during which time I almost totally isolated myself from the world and turned the one thing I had always loved into something very dangerous.

For some years, the eating disorder was my way of coping with life and when bad became worse, I just didn't want to go on, but my family and those around me encouraged me to seek help. I moved back home to the countryside, began counselling, acupuncture and alternative therapies, and I was lucky enough to have good support, which ultimately saved my life.

I tried so many things and after years with a great counsellor, there was a moment when I suddenly realized that I really did want to change. This had to come from within and what came was my need to rebuild positive relationships

– not only with food, but with those around me, my lifestyle and more specifically my understanding of and relationship to my mind. I wanted to learn how to live in a way that would enable me to manage my moods, find stability and passion through nurturing my mental health.

To do this, I unlocked a new toolbox of ingredients. I found food that firstly, I didn't have issues with, but also ingredients that I knew were deeply nourishing and could help me come back to life as I once knew it. My diet was not plant-based at the time, but I realized that there were a few foods that weren't agreeing with my then weak body. Plants and tonic herbs sparked a new passion and I ended up spending the last part of my degree writing what was to become the first draft for this book – *The Recipe for Wellbeing* was to be a lifestyle trend book outlining a rebrand of mental health with a trend for Mind Food. This book led me to start working in the food industry, as well as becoming the blueprint for my own recovery.

I started to really explore this reignited passion and began working part time in some great food places. On completing my degree I began retraining as a chef, specifically in plant-based food, and setting out on a new path to find a way to connect everyone with the links between plant-based food and mental health. From then on, things seemed to align and completely unexpectedly, I was asked to be involved in the opening of an incredible restaurant named Asparagasm, which enabled me to bring this food dream to life. It led to valuable years spent creating recipes, designing menus and working at pop-up events and festivals, which gave me so much in terms of understanding food as art, food for different people, functional food, raw food, vegan food, gluten-free food and zero-waste cooking.

Looking back over this time, I was not quite fully recovered from my eating disorder, but all these experiences were stepping stones to making it. Historically, when things in my life became challenging, as they do at times for everyone, my eating has been the first thing to suffer. Slowly, over time, I have understood these triggers and have

transformed my relationship with food. Now as well as having a variety of practices, tools and techniques that really help, which I have outlined in this book for you to try, I can easily manage such anxieties before they become problems.

From Asparagasm I travelled the world teaching plant-based food to professional chefs and aspiring foodies and now have various projects of my own such as Plant Academy, my cookery school, The Food Studio, which is a space co-created with Sara who is also the photographer for this book, and a food consultancy business, always finding ways to work with brands and individuals to bring dreams to life through food and share the Mind Food mindset.

There have been times in the last decade that I have wanted to write this book, but it always felt like, as society, we weren't quite ready and it's only recently that mental health, its relationship with food and brain care have become more mainstream and hugely relevant to everyone, particularly with the huge challenges of isolation that the Covid-19 pandemic has forced upon people in so many countries around the world. We are ready now to think differently about mental health, but there is still a long way to go. The pandemic helped the world to slow down, and although devastating, mental health specifically has now become more widely spoken about. People tend to be more open to lifestyle remedies that can support general health in addition to mental health.

We saw how a pandemic can mobilize society and it is time that we did the same for mental health. *Mind Food* is a step in giving you ideas and knowledge but there are many more steps to go. The more we prioritize curating our own lives in a mind-nourishing way, the more society will follow suit.

Unfortunately, current society is set up in a way that isn't supportive of a Mind Food life but we can implement practices to support the mind, eliminate distress and set boundaries to help get us there.

Reflecting on my past experiences, I now know that it's only since I really implemented all these techniques and took time to slow down a little that my mental health has really improved long term. I'm extremely grateful that I had all these tools, ideas, research and connections, which have helped me to get to this place and it really is my passion and mission to share these ideas further, make them more accessible, desirable and mainstream. So much of this comes down to how we choose to live and building knowledge and resilience into our society, so together we can live in a way that will enable us all to feed our minds.

HOW THIS BOOK WORKS

Mind Food is not just the ingredients we use, but the act of coming together around a table to share more than food. It's about connecting with others and the world around us, as well as delving deeper within yourself. This book is a toolbox of ideas that you can use every day of your life. The recipes in this book are designed to be interesting, yet simple to make. You will find new flavours, try uplifting recipes and hopefully glimpse an alternative mindset that might change the way you experience your own mental health and the wider world.

The main dishes, breakfasts and lunch recipes are split into the four seasons. These recipes are created not only to taste delicious, but also to take your mind to a different place. Think of them as a moving meditation, where the result is something delicious, together with a good dose of headspace. If you aren't confident in the kitchen, try the shorter recipes first and as your confidence builds, work your way up to make the longer recipes.

There is a long chapter on desserts, my favourite topic, laced with tonic herbs; Mind Food is as much about treats and enjoying food as anything else! The drinks chapter is where I share more ideas on herbs for mental health, with a selection of straightforward and tasty recipes for teas, tonics and tipples. You will also find a full section on pantry staples like candied nuts, nut butters and salty seeds to add to your dishes, which can be made once and last for ages. This is a good place to start as they are easy to add to your favourite dishes.

A key part of brain health is looking after the gut, so you can find more information on fermented food and the gut to brain connection on page 160, with a selection of straightforward and totally tasty ferments to try.

There is also a chapter designed to help you with batch cooking, written to assist if you simply need a dressing idea, want to make your own plant-based milk or prepare for the week ahead. You will also find a sample weekly plan towards the end of the book (see page 170) that I hope will help you get started with batch cooking.

I have taken inspiration from my own food experiences, training and travels so must say that some recipes are an adaptation of a traditional dish. I do this with full respect to these diverse and totally inspiring cultures and share this ancient wisdom with the addition of modern Mind Food ideas.

Mindset

Mind Food is as much about the headspace we are in as what we cook. You can always taste if there aren't good vibes put into what you eat, so when cooking, always try to be in the zone and make cooking fun, whether alone or with friends and family around.

The longer recipes in this book can help you to take your mind away from other concerns in your life and provide something different to think about and focus on, even for just a little while. Regular mindfulness and meditation, in whatever form, can help each one of us to feel a more general sense of calm, day to day.

Food is an international language that brings people together, and is one thing which we can all relate to and connect with, a fantastic way of expressing yourself and connecting with others. Explore the different ways in which creating *Mind Food* recipes and cooking work for you. Some days you might feel sociable, others meditative or creative. I hope that the recipes in this book bring different feelings to your days and weeks ahead, and progressively, that you find making them a useful addition to your life.

THE LANGUAGE OF MIND FOOD

You will see that each recipe is given a mood to guide you through your own Mind Food experience. There are simple ingredient swaps and tips that indicate how you can tweak the recipe to suit your own individual needs.

SOOTHE

These recipes will hopefully bring a little comfort to you. They are warm and foster a feeling of cosiness, and can help you to feel more grounded. Think of warm spices, roasted flavours and familiar scents that may bring that feeling to you.

CHILL

Our chill recipes bring about a sense of calm, and most often contain tonic herbs and smooth flavours that can help you to unwind and relax.

LIFT

Lift recipes bring a spring to your step. They are slightly fiery and bright, so if you need energy, look for a 'lift'.

BALANCE

Balance meals are wholesome and will give you energy but also ground you. If you're looking for deep nourishment, balance is exactly what you need.

FOCUS

Focus recipes are for those moments when you need to be on the ball. If you need to think about a creative project or concentrate on a particular task, look for 'focus'.

This is not a prescription.
We're all on a spectrum of mental health and although there isn't just one 'recipe' that works for everyone, you do need to be open minded as any one of these ideas might just be the one that is right for you. Unless something is prescribed for us, we often brush it off, but there are some easily accessible everyday things that can help everyone.

Exploring the ideas and recipes contained in this book may just lead you to meet someone or encounter something that you can relate to; that someone or something might be able to shed new light on a situation you are experiencing.

If you are suffering from a severe mental health issue, work with your current practitioner to get guidance on making any changes. Just because a condition is not visible, doesn't mean it's not serious. It's always advisable to seek professional help when you are dealing with any mental health issue. If you do need further support, I have included further information and resources on page 191.

This book was reviewed by a Registered Dietitian Nutritionist and uses ingredients that research has shown to be beneficial to mental health, but it's not a research study. For further information on the science behind these ingredients, visit my website which lists sources on Mind Food (www.laurenlovatt.com).

INGREDIENTS

ON THE WHOLE, Mind Food ingredients are eaten in their natural form not only because unprocessed ingredients optimize taste and nutrition, but because when you start any recipe with good ingredients, you can't go far wrong.

As *Mind Food* is written with the four seasons in mind, I strongly encourage you to shop as locally and seasonally as possible. Support independent shops where you can, and if you are able to choose organic food and local growers, the flavours on your plate and the feeling you will experience after your meals will be greatly improved. The seasonal ingredients in the book are meant to be fleeting and savoured for their brief seasonal charm. No matter where in the world you live, try to work within the seasons and cycles of the environment you live in.

Using seasonal ingredients has meant, in addition to using fewer exotic fruits and nuts, I have enjoyed exploring ingredients that are less familiar and are more readily available closer to home. This has led me to discover many new ingredients, such as hemp seeds, Aztec broccoli, peacock kale and even things like carob, which have a lower carbon footprint. Of course, you will still find things like cacao and medicinal herbs in the book but I try to be more conscious about how often they are used and where they come from.

I know this way of shopping may not be accessible to everyone, but it is something I hope we all aspire to and that you take your own small steps to make useful improvements in your shopping. If you are buying ingredients from larger shops or supermarkets, check the back of the packet of anything that has been processed. There are often ingredients that aren't conducive to good mental health or health in general and it's easy to be caught out. The signs I look out for are excessive stabilizers and gums, maltodextrin, vegetable oils and MSG, which can cause issues or irritate problems you may already have. Often food labels begin with the predominant ingredient, so if it lists sugar or something unexpected first on the list, the product may not be so great. Taking that moment just to check the label carefully can prevent wasted money on something that isn't helpful or particularly healthy long term.

The recipes you find in the book are 100 per cent plant-based, not because I believe we should all eat in a certain way, but because by understanding these ideas and finding fantastic flavours through fruit and vegetables, you will hopefully see how satisfying this way of eating can be. I believe that plant-based food and Mind Food do go hand in hand, as the better our mental health, the better the state of the planet.

Some *Mind Food* star ingredients are especially useful in supporting our mental health. As you will see in the recipes, it is sometimes the ingredient combinations and flavours that create a certain vibe in a dish and will take your mood and mind to a different, and hopefully positive, place. These recipes are intended to be part of your life longterm. Mind Food is about balance, having exactly what you want when you want it, but being conscious enough to know what makes you feel good and what your body needs.

Leafy Greens

Kale, spinach, spring greens, dandelion greens and any edible plant with a dark green leaf are extremely important for looking after our brains. These green leafy vegetables are nutrient dense and deeply nourishing for our overall health and especially our brains. Leafy greens are rich in brain-healthy nutrients like vitamin K, lutein, folate and beta carotene. Research suggests eating leafy greens may help slow cognitive decline, so they should grace our Mind Food plates at least once a day.

Rainbow Vegetables

Diversity is key in the plants we eat and plays a huge part in a balanced and healthy lifestyle. Each variety of multicoloured vegetable has unique benefits that support our minds in different ways. In *Mind Food*, I prioritize a wide variety of veg and try to introduce you to plenty of unique varieties too, like kalettes, wild mushrooms and seaweeds to name a few. Noting what colours are missing from your diet can be a useful assessment tool when deciding what foods to add in or try. Aim for 10 different plants every day and at least 30 across the week for optimum biodiversity and brain support.

Fruit

In *Mind Food*, we celebrate berries as they are rich in antioxidants and polyphenols, in addition to which, they happen to be one of the most well-studied brain-positive ingredients. A diet rich in berries leads to profound long-term benefits on our brains. Research at Harvard's Brigham and Women's Hospital found that women who consumed two or more servings of blueberries and strawberries each week delayed memory decline by up to two-and-a-half years. Including about 60g (½ cup) of berries every day in your diet is particularly beneficial to brain health. Find recipe inspiration in the smoothies on page 119, Antioxidant Jam on page 154 and throughout the desserts chapter on pages 120–145.

Whole Grains

The whole grains you will find used most in this book are black rice, short grain brown rice, oats, buckwheat and quinoa (which are technically seeds but used similarly to a grain within a dish). These grains are rich in fibre, which is vital for optimum digestion, as well as a variety of beneficial minerals. Cold carbs, like cooked and cooled rice, are also a great source of prebiotics, so you will find we sometimes use properly cooled grains to make something else.

A note on oats: throughout the book, I have kept the recipes gluten free. Gluten might be something that doesn't suit you, and it's always worth investigating as gluten intolerances and coeliac disease are ever more common and can be a source of irritation and major health issues. If you can't eat any type of oats, you can use millet, brown rice or quinoa flakes in place of them – they work well in all of the recipes that use oats.

Beans

Chickpeas, adzuki beans, black beans, butter beans and so many more go much further than just being an excellent source of protein, B vitamins and fibre. Beans in *Mind Food* are used to create creamy sauces and cookie dough, for example, and black beans especially are one of my favourite mood-boosting foods. You will find out more about them in the Kimchi and Black Bean Tostadas recipe on page 59 and the Sprouted Chickpea Hummus on page 176.

Healthy Fats

Healthy fats are a key point of brain care as the brain is made up of 60 per cent fat. Just like any other part of the body, the brain needs specific nutrients for optimum function, and healthy fats are a crucial part of this way of eating. Olive oil, nuts, seeds and avocados are great ingredients filled with good fats.

In *Mind Food*, I suggest using cold-pressed oils, using mainly olive oil for its antioxidant benefits in dressings, desserts and in cooking. You will also find that sesame oil, hemp oil and, on the very rare occasion, sunflower oil are used for frying, but not something recommended in high quantities.

Eating 3 tablespoons of olive oil a day is said to have brain-boosting benefits as found in the SMILES trial – one of the most widely recognized research studies on the positive effects of a healthy diet on our mental health. There are huge debates concerning oils and, from my point of view, everything is best in moderation. As far as oils are concerned, quality is key and it being organic and unrefined is so important, so do try to shop wisely.

Seeds

Seeds are a wonderful source of healthy fats and unique nutrients that support our brains. Hemp is our hero seed known for its brain-boosting properties since it is omega rich. You will find a wide selection of hemp recipes from Hemp Milk and Hemp Yoghurt (see page 171) to That CBD Caramel Shortbread (see page 130) and many more.

Seeds are also known to support female hormones in particular, and in the recipe for Lunar Cookies on page 128, you will learn about seed syncing for the female monthly cycle. Hormone imbalances can be a cause of poor mental health and making use of this natural support system can make a world of difference.

Nuts

The incredible selection of good-quality nuts out there are full of good fats and vitamin E, which can also help with concentration, together with their unique flavours and general goodness. Our Mind Food nut of choice is the brain-nourishing walnut, which coincidentally looks like a brain, and has a high concentration of ALA (alpha-linolenic acid), a plant-based omega-3 fatty acid. Pistachios are also known to be brain-supporting.

Soy

Soy products can be beneficial in small doses, especially when fermented, and you will therefore find tempeh, miso and tamari within the *Mind Food* recipes. Soy is also known to be a source of tryptophan, which aids serotonin production, helping with focus and supporting a good night's sleep. Again, choose the best-quality soy that you can, as quality is key.

Fermented Foods

These foods are such a crucial part of our mental health, because of the gut-brain connection. As our knowledge increases around the microbiome, so do the clear links to and benefits of supporting our gut health in order to enable our mental health to improve. We are all familiar with the term 'gut feeling' or 'getting butterflies in our stomach', and you will recognize we often use the gut to describe emotions. The research out there in the public domain is proving this exciting connection more and more. You will find more information about this in the fermentation section of the book (see pages 160–169) and I suggest that you experience it for yourself with recipes like the Kombucha Chimichurri (see page 175).

Herbs and Spices

Turmeric, saffron, cinnamon, ginger, chilli, oregano, sage and rosemary are some of my favourite herbs to use in Mind Food recipes, not only for their fantastic flavours, but also for their health benefits. Each herb contains many compounds known to help with a variety of problems such as reducing inflammation, promoting neurogenesis, improving blood flow and boosting our moods. Including small amounts of a wide variety of herbs and spices will always do something good for the flavour of your food and the power of your mind.

Salt

The salt used in *Mind Food* is flaked sea salt or Pink Himalayan salt. I also use tamari and miso in recipes where a little extra salt is needed. These salts are unrefined and are used in small amounts to keep us in balance.

Sweeteners

The sweeteners used in *Mind Food* recipes are as unrefined as possible. You will find honey, dates, maple syrup, rapadura sugar (a whole unrefined cane sugar) and molasses. They are used for their unique flavours and I recommend that you explore different options, rather than the more commonly used and more refined white sugar and agave.

Tonic Herbs and Plants

Medicinal mushrooms, maca and ashwagandha are some of the more potent plants that appear throughout this book. Using food as medicine is part of what Mind Food is all about, so I encourage you to explore these powerful plants and find which ones resonate with you. You will find them used mostly in the drinks chapter (see pages 108–119) and the desserts chapter (see pages 120–145).

CBD

CBD oil, or cannibidoil, is a chemical compound extracted from the leaves and flowers of the hemp plant. It works with the endocannabinoid system to activate receptors in the brain that control things like mood and temperature, helping you restore your natural balance. Delve deeper into CBD and there's a whole world of scientific research taking place, from Harvard and MIT to King's College London. There are also hundreds of testimonials from people using CBD to treat conditions like epilepsy, Parkinson's, insomnia and anxiety.

We know that omega-rich hemp products are shown to reduce inflammation, blood pressure and the jitters from caffeine, but CBD is also linked to mental health, and has been reported to reduce anxiety and depression in a number of different cases. All the recipes here are designed to make you feel good and CBD can support this feeling of calm. You will see CBD in many of the Mind Food savoury recipes, dressings, drinks and desserts. Quality is key with CBD: personally, I like Good Hemp, Hempen or Ho Karan. It is important to start with a smaller dose and see how you feel.

Cacao

The recipes in this book use cacao rather than cocoa. Cacao pods grow most commonly in Africa, Asia and South America. When they are ripe, they are taken from the tree and cracked open to reveal their seeds, which look like lychees, and inside each fruity pod there is a soft bean. Raw cacao is left to ferment and as the skin and seeds dry they become cacao beans. The beans are then cracked open to show the nibs, which are ground into cacao paste, butter and powder. Cacao is less processed, much tastier and more nutrient dense than cocoa. You can of course use cocoa if you can't get cacao, but please ensure that it is ethically sourced. The origin and quality of the cacao beans will affect how much you benefit from consuming them.

Water

Our brains are made of 75–80 per cent water and hydration is a key pillar of our health. It is known that even slight dehydration can cause changes in memory and attention span, while also making the brain work harder than normal.

It must be noted that as one may expect with other ingredients, the quality of the water used in all recipes is key. Water quality can affect taste in cooking and can gradually negatively impact your health. I always filter water, using either a charcoal stick, which removes any impurities and is a very cost-effective filter system, or a water filter in the form of a small tank, jug or addition to the tap. Water quality varies and you may find your local tap water benefits from being filtered. If this is the case for you, it may be worth researching in order to make the most out of your own water supply for cooking and drinking.

It is also important to know that hydration does not only come from water. Water predominantly helps to flush the system. Herbal infusions, fermented drinks and nut milks can also be a beneficial part of brain health. You can find some inspiration in the drinks chapter (see pages 108–119).

FORGET ABOUT SUPERFOODS

I really wanted to make the recipes in Mind Food as straightforward and inexpensive as possible, but I also wanted to share the optimum way in which these recipes can be made, so you will see that many of the medicinal plants we use here are optional. As much as I don't like the term 'superfoods', these medicinal plant powders can be thought perhaps unnecessary as they can be a little expensive and may come from further afield. But if sourced wisely, ingredients like maca, ashwagandha and medicinal mushrooms are useful and can have incredibly potent effects.

Although not essential, I have noticed the monumental impact things like medicinal mushrooms can have on our mental health. I wouldn't run out and get them all but introduce them one by one to your recipes, and remember you only need a small amount, often only up to a teaspoon a day, of your chosen plant. There is no point having too much or making too much of a cocktail of these tonic herbs as we can only absorb so much.

ORGANIC

Organic food occasionally gets bad press for its price, but organic food is simply food as it should be, in its natural form with nothing additional that will harm either ourselves or the environment. Organic food doesn't need to be certified to be organic, and if you conduct a little research, visit farmers' markets and really see what you are buying, it's often a very inexpensive way of eating. If you can connect closer to the source of your food, by being curious and supporting more independent shops, your food quality will no doubt improve, as well as the flavour of your meals. With all produce in this book I recommend prioritizing local ingredients. If you buy an organic mango that has been shipped across the world, its potency and taste will be diminished, not to mention its green credentials. Plus, the more we demand organic, the more accessible and inexpensive it will become – another opportunity to vote with your fork.

A NOTE ON ANIMAL PROTEIN

Mind Food is entirely entwined with sustainable eating. I found plants to be easier on my weak body when I was in recovery, which was an important factor in why I became plant based. There are major benefits in eating a biodiverse range of plants – more than 30 a week – as biodiversity is crucial to the health of our gut. Plant-based eating deeply nourishes our bodies and our minds so the recipes in this book put a wide range of plants at the centre of the table.

At the time I am writing this we individually and collectively have the opportunity to make a huge difference to the climate crisis and while this issue can feel hugely overwhelming we know that prioritizing plants on our plates can have a monumental positive impact on our climate, as the food system has the single biggest impact on the planet. To make this less overwhelming, the recipes in this book are all created to be planet friendly and I hope that as you start to taste this concept you will see new ways to enjoy making your personal contribution through your plate.

There are many different schools of thought in the use of animals in our food systems and as with any subject I encourage you to do your own research and feel what resonates with you. It has been said that fish is useful for brain health and there can be benefits to your mental health if you include it in your meals, prioritizing wild-caught oily fish over anything else. If you are not eating fish it is very important to to ensure you get omega-3, either by means of a supplement or derived from algae. Seaweeds can be a useful source of omega-3 for plant-based diets.

Each small decision we make can have an impact on ourselves and the world around us. No one is too great or too small to make an impact, and I find it extremely empowering to know that you can do this yourself through each bite. We are all learning each day what works for us individually, and however your plate looks now, you can start from where you are and make small changes each day, at your own pace, knowing that each one is a step in the right direction for your own mental health and beyond.

SPRING

Spring is a time when things are ready to grow. The days lighten up and hopefully the temperatures get a little bit warmer. Spring is also a time for enjoying a bounty of greens, berries and sprouts as they burst into life even more. This is also the best time for eating lighter, raw-centric meals full of the superb ingredients on offer.

Spring is the moment we often think about a spring clean or refresh and is the perfect time to shake up our own routine by perhaps cleaning out things we no longer need. I love to add a new practice to my yoga or meditation routine, change my meal times and get outside as much as possible to soak up the slowly emerging sunshine.

During this time of year, particularly as the sun comes out and the days become longer, I find many days become even more full with time torn between work and home life. It's the time when we can feel more energized and may want to do more than we have in previous months to prepare ahead, enjoy the new produce and soak up the fresh spring air.

INGREDIENTS FOR SPRING

SPROUTING

Sprouting literally means to bring a seed to life. The process of sprouting makes the seed more easily digestible and more nutritious. There are three ways you can sprout:

1. In the jar
This method is best for broccoli sprouts, alfalfa sprouts, radish, beans or legumes. Simply add 4 tbsp of your chosen seeds to a 1l jar with 1 cup of water. Leave the seeds to soak for at least 6 hours or overnight, then rinse them in a sieve. Place the seeds back into the jar with a piece of kitchen paper covering the top of the jar, sealed with an elastic band. Find an ambient place for your sprouting seeds, such as a shelf out of direct sunlight. Repeat the rinsing process morning and evening, and within a day or two you will see the sprouts start to grow. For alfalfa and radish, they will be ready when the top blooms into a colourful shoot.

For legumes, the tail of the sprout should not exceed the length of the bean, which will take 3–5 days.

2. The kitchen paper method
This is the best option for seeds like chia, camelina and cress. Place a piece of wet kitchen paper on a plate, then sprinkle on the seeds, aiming for an even coverage. The seeds can be close together but not overlapping too much. Cover the base plate with an upside down plate to keep the atmosphere humid. Each morning and evening make sure the towel is moist by sprinkling it with water and after a few days you will see the sprouts start to grow. Leave to grow for 5–10 days until they are green and a few inches high, when they will be ready to harvest and enjoy.

3. Sow the seeds
This method of sprouting is best for pea shoots, buckwheat and other similar grasses. Start the same way as in the jar method, soaking and sprouting your chosen seeds for a few days. When they are sprouted, fill a suitable waterproof container with 1 inch of soil. Make sure this is big enough for your seeds to spread out in. Plant the sprouted seeds on top and cover with another thin layer of soil, then water. Keep this moist every morning and evening for a couple of weeks until the sprouts have grown 2–5 inches.

MOVEMENT

Much research has been done in the last 10 years into the benefits of fitness, not only for our physical health, but also for our mental health. There are the more obvious effects of how physical activity can increase our self-esteem as we feel fitter and stronger, but we also know that just 10 minutes of physical exercise a day can reduce stress and improve sleep. Like all practices in *Mind Food*, there is not a one-size-fits-all approach: it's about knowing the options and exploring what works for you.

It's worth remembering that physical exercise doesn't have to be overly physical – walking can have a monumental impact on our minds and I often find if I make time for a long walk, I discover new ideas and a much calmer state of mind. The best place to start is by not being too hard on yourself, aiming to try one new thing each week to get started. There are so many activities to try, from dancing, climbing, yoga and cycling, to qigong, swimming, surfing or sprinting – persevere until something clicks with you and know it will be a step towards better mental health.

SOUND HEALING

This is becoming more well-known in the West, and we need it more when we are out of tune with our natural cycles. Sound healing involves using crystal or metal bowls with various instruments to retune our body frequency. You can find sound healing experiences around the world and online. These normally involve laying down in a warm room and going on the 'sound journey'. This practice is said to ease energetic blockages, bringing the body back into harmony by producing vibrations that alter our brainwaves. My first sound healing journey was pretty transformative and my head definitely felt much clearer afterwards.

OMEGA SEEDS AND ANCIENT OAT BIRCHER

These overnight oats are designed to bring a moment of calm to any morning. When we are looking to bring balance to our brains, eating a simple breakfast within an hour of waking up is a good idea. These oats can be eaten alone or topped with seasonal fruits. You can also add a tablespoon of bee pollen for extra sweetness and a little buzz.

Serves: 2

Time taken: 5 minutes,
    plus overnight

300ml (1¼ cups) Hemp Milk
    (see page 171), or any plant-based milk
100g (1 cup) gluten-free oats
2 tbsp chia seeds
50g (¼ cup) hemp seeds
1 tbsp honey
½ tsp vanilla extract
¼ tsp pink Himalayan salt
1 tbsp rose water (optional)
1 tsp ashwagandha (optional)
1 pipette CBD (optional)

Add all of the ingredients to a medium glass jar or bowl and whisk with a fork. Leave to sit for a few minutes and then whisk again – this will prevent the chia seeds from sticking together. If you have time, whisk every few minutes for ten minutes for the optimum results.

Place the oat bircher mixture in the fridge overnight and enjoy the next morning topped with fresh fruit, hemp yoghurt and bee pollen.

TIP – Have you heard of ashwagandha? The name comes from Sanskrit and is said to impart the 'strength of a horse' as it is regarded as one of the most powerful healing substances in Ayurveda (see page 67). Ashwagandha most commonly comes in powdered form and is a nootropic, which means that it can improve cognitive function and provide a lot of neurological nourishment. Plus, its unique make up is said to help serotonin production for an improved mood and resilience to stress.

WILD GREENS AND GRAINS

Whole Lettuce Salad

At this time of year, there is an abundance of greenery. This whole lettuce dish is such a satisfying lunch with its many dressings, whole grains and seeds. Get stuck in, wrap and roll the leaves with the sauces and have fun – salad definitely doesn't need to live up to its boring stereotype!

Serves: 2
Time taken: 10 minutes

1 whole butter lettuce
200g (generous 1 cup) cooked quinoa
50g (⅓ cup) pistachios
30g (⅓ cup) fresh parsley, chopped
100g (3½oz) Hot Sauce
    (see page 174)
100ml (3½fl oz) Herb Stem Vinaigrette,
    (see page 177)

For the lemon tahini
100g (½ cup) tahini
50ml (scant ¼ cup) lemon juice
50ml (scant ¼ cup) water
50ml (scant ¼ cup) olive oil
1 tsp turmeric
¼ tsp salt
⅛ tsp dried chilli flakes

Preheat the oven to 170°C fan (190°C/375°F/Gas 5). Once hot, place the pistachios on a small baking tray and roast for 10 minutes to lightly release their nutty aroma. Once roasted, remove the pistachios from the oven and leave them to cool.

GREENS Wash the lettuce by submerging it in water and making sure it is thoroughly cleaned. Remove it from the water and cut off the base, keeping the rest of the lettuce intact. Leave the lettuce to dry while you make the other elements.

LEMON TAHINI Blend or whisk all of the ingredients together until smooth and store in a jar in the fridge until ready to serve.

GRAINS Heat a frying pan with a splash of oil and lightly toast the already-cooked quinoa for 10 minutes, until golden and crisp. After that time, turn off the heat and add the parsley with a little extra salt and pepper.

While the quinoa toasts, roughly chop the pistachios, leaving some larger pieces so you discover different textures as you eat.

To serve, place a circle of lemon tahini on the plate followed by the sizzling quinoa and then the lettuce. Lightly drizzle the lettuce with the Hot Sauce, Herb Stem Vinaigrette and pistachios. Serve to share as a vibrant green lunch or as part of a spring spread.

TIP – You can use any bountiful lettuce here. Butter lettuce works really well raw with its wonderfully crisp and creamy leaves, but if you have something like baby gem, you can try heating a griddle pan and griddling it lightly to enhance the flavour. Other good varieties for a springtime feast include Batavia or Frisée.

SUNSHINE ON A PLATE

Vegetable Tumbet

This tumbet holds a special place in my food memories, as for many years my family visited a restaurant in Mallorca called El Siller, where I was first introduced to the beauty of farm to fork food. The restaurant was owned by a Spanish farmer and his wife, who grew all of their own vegetables on their farm and served a small, totally seasonal menu. This experience made me realize the massive difference that simple but good ingredients make, not just to the taste, but to how you feel.

Serves: 2
Time taken: 1 hour

For the tumbet

1 aubergine (eggplant)
1 large potato
50ml (scant ¼ cup) olive oil
1 tbsp salt

For the oregano arrabbiata

2 tbsp olive oil
1 red onion, finely chopped
1 tsp salt
1 garlic clove, peeled and crushed
1 fresh red chilli, deseeded and finely sliced
1 tbsp smoked paprika
400ml (1⅔ cups) passata
1 tbsp dried oregano
1 sprig rosemary

To serve

1 courgette (zucchini), peeled into thin ribbons
1 batch of Hemp and Parsley Pesto
   (see page 175) or your favourite
   store-bought pesto
Sea salt
Freshly cracked black pepper
Handful of herbs, such as basil or parsley

Preheat the oven to 180°C fan (200°C/400°F/Gas 6).

VEGETABLES Slice each of the tumbet vegetables into 5mm (¼in) rounds, making sure they are all even, as this will greatly affect the end result. Take your time here.

You will need 2 large baking trays to lay out the vegetables. Drizzle each tray with a very generous amount of olive oil and a pinch of salt, then place the potato on one tray and the aubergine on the other, as this may take a little less time to cook. Rub each vegetable round in the salt and oil so that they are well covered. Spread them out flat over the trays and bake for at least 30 minutes, turning the vegetables over after 15 minutes, until they are golden brown.

OREGANO ARRABBIATA Meanwhile, heat a saucepan with the olive oil and add the onion and salt. Cook over a very low heat for at least 10 minutes until cooked and soft but not too golden. Once the onion is cooked, add the garlic and chilli and cook for a further 2 minutes to release their wonderful aroma. Then add the smoked paprika and cook for 1 more minute.

Add the passata to the pan with an equal amount of water, then add the oregano and rosemary and cook to reduce the sauce for 20 minutes until it is thick and silky, stirring every now and then to make sure the sauce isn't sticking to the base of the pan. You will know it is ready when the sauce is thick and has the fragrance of herbs.

To serve, toss the courgette ribbons in a little oil and salt. Place a spoonful of smoking hot arrabbiata onto your plate, followed by vegetables delicately layered with spoonfuls of pesto in between each one. Finish with the courgette ribbons, salt, freshly cracked black pepper and a handful of your favourite herbs and enjoy!

CBD STIR-FRY

At this time of year, I love cooking dishes that I can throw together. All of the elements from this stir-fry last for a good amount of time and take just a little prep work. The best part of this dish is perhaps the wild rice, which is in fact not a rice at all. I discovered this way of 'blooming' wild rice a few years ago when I was teaching in Barcelona and I've been taken by it ever since. A great way to increase variety in your meals is to include less common plants and the 'rice' provides a totally different nutty texture and technique to this dish.

Serves: 2

Time taken: 30 minutes,
    plus overnight sprouting

150g (generous ¾ cup) wild rice

1 tbsp sesame oil

250g (9oz) purple sprouting or
    regular stem broccoli,
    woody ends removed

1 carrot, peeled and ribboned

¼ of a medium red cabbage, finely sliced

1 red chilli, chopped and deseeded

1 garlic clove, peeled

2.5cm (1in) piece of fresh ginger

50g (1¾oz) sunflower or
    pumpkin seeds, to serve

2 pipettes CBD

For the satay sauce

100g (generous ½ cup) almond or
    peanut butter

3 tbsp tamari

1 tbsp toasted sesame oil

1 tbsp lion's mane mushroom powder
    (optional)

Juice of 1 lime

1 tbsp fresh red chilli, chopped

1 tsp honey (optional)

RICE 'Bloom' the wild rice the day before you want to eat this dish. Place the wild rice in a food processor to 'score' it.

Place the scored rice into a large bowl or container and cover it generously with water. Make sure the container is big enough for the rice to double its size. Cover the rice with a cloth or loose-fitting lid and leave for 12 hours at room temperature. You will notice the rice blooms quite quickly and you will see it curl and then soften. When the rice is significantly softer and curled it is ready to use. If you are not using it right away, you can drain it from the soaking water and store it in the fridge for up to 5 days.

SATAY SAUCE Make the satay sauce by blending all of the ingredients together with 50ml (¼ cup) water until smooth. You may need to add a splash more water so you have a thick but pourable consistency, depending on the thickness of the nut butter.

STIR-FRY Cook the stir-fry by heating a large griddle pan with the sesame oil and, once hot, adding the vegetables. Sizzle until each one is cooked through; if your broccoli is slightly on the thicker side, add 2 tablespoons of water to the pan to help it steam and cook through. Add the drained bloomed rice and chopped chilli, and grate over the garlic and ginger. Cook for a further minute or two to release the aroma and thoroughly heat the rice.

To serve, add a spoonful of satay sauce to the plate, top with a few spoonfuls of the stir-fry and sprinkle over the seeds and the CBD oil.

SIZZLING COURGETTES WITH TZATZIKI

These courgettes are a real crowd pleaser – simple yet very effective. We teach this dish at the Plant Academy, and it goes down a treat. As someone who enjoys lighter lunches, this dish really hits the spot and is packed full of ingredients that bring energy to any spring day.

Serves: 2
Time taken: 30 minutes

1 large courgette (zucchini)
2 tbsp olive oil
Pinch of salt

For the tzatziki
200g (1 cup) plant-based yoghurt
200g (7oz) cucumber, grated
 (about half a cucumber)
1 garlic clove
10g (⅓oz) parsley, finely chopped
¼ tsp salt

To serve
Handful of your favourite candied seeds
 (see page 69)
4 tbsp Kombucha Chimichurri
 (see page 175)
Small bunch of fresh pea shoots or
 watercress

TZATZIKI Make the tzatziki by mixing together all of the ingredients in a small bowl. Set to one side until needed.

COURGETTES The key thing for this recipe is to cut the courgette into perfect fillets. To do this, cut the courgette into three 5cm (2in) pieces. Cut each piece into three, lengthwise, moving around the seeds. We are looking for even fillets here. Cross-hatch each fillet evenly.

Heat a frying pan with the olive oil until hot and add the courgette fillets, skin-side-up. Cook over a medium heat until beautifully golden, then flip onto the skin side until the fillets are cooked through.

To serve, place the tzatziki in three or five dots on the plate. Lay each fillet on the dots, then sprinkle a few candied seeds on each courgette, drizzle with Kombucha Chimichurri and garnish with leaves.

"And the day came where the risk to remain tight in the bud was more painful than the risk it took to blossom"

—Anaïs Nin

THE ULTIMATE KIMCHI CURRY

This bowl is inspired by the many trips that I have made to Bali, which is a place that has gone a long way to showing me a different pace of life and the power of ceremony, always with fantastic colours and a balance of flavours to experience. I will always remember my first trip there, trying their nasi goreng and nasi campur dishes, which include bites of rice, vegetables and delicious sauces, often served with tasty tempeh, which is a Mind Food sort of superfood!

Serves: 4

Time taken: 45 minutes

150g (generous ¾ cup) red or black rice,
    soaked for 8 hours, then rinsed thoroughly

For the sizzling tempeh

50ml (scant ¼ cup) tamari

50ml (scant ¼ cup) sesame oil

2 tbsp lime juice

1 tsp chilli powder

150g (5½oz) tempeh, chopped into
    even pieces

For the curry

1 tbsp sesame oil

1 red onion, peeled and finely sliced

1 garlic clove, peeled and finely grated

2.5cm (1in) piece of fresh ginger, finely grated

1 tsp curry powder

100g (⅔ cup) kimchi

1 × 400ml (14fl oz) tin of coconut milk

200ml (scant 1 cup) passata

Handful of spring greens, kale or spinach

2 large carrots, peeled and chopped into
    evenly-sized pieces

10g (⅛ cup) dulse seaweed

For the crispy kale

100g kale (3½oz), whole small leaves

100g (3½oz) chickpea flour + 50g (1¾oz)
    for dusting

1 tbsp curry powder

½ tsp salt

125ml (4¼fl oz) sparkling water

200ml (7fl oz) sunflower oil

To serve

3-4 tbsp plant-based yoghurt (I like coconut)

30g (⅓ cup) coriander

TIP – If you can't find tempeh,
try using a firm tofu. Both are good
sources of protein, which is a vital
part of a Mind Food life.

RICE Cook the soaked red or black rice in a saucepan covered in plenty of water, then bring to the boil. Once boiling, reduce the heat and simmer for 35 minutes while you complete the remaining steps.

TEMPEH In a small container, whisk together the tamari, sesame oil, lime juice and chilli powder, then add the tempeh. Make sure each piece is evenly covered and leave to marinate.

CURRY Place a large saucepan on the heat and add the sesame oil. When the oil is hot, add the sliced onion and cook with a pinch of salt for 10 minutes until soft and very lightly coloured. Now add the garlic, ginger, curry powder and half of the kimchi, and cook for a further minute. Add the coconut milk and passata and leave over a low heat for the flavours to infuse. Add the spring greens to the saucepan with the carrots and dulse seaweed and leave them to wilt.

TEMPEH Place a frying pan over high heat and, when it is hot, add the tempeh. Fry the tempeh on both sides until it is crisp and golden.

KALE Wash the kale, keeping the leaves whole, and then pat dry. Whisk the chickpea flour, curry powder, salt and sparkling water until smooth.

Now set up another bowl with the extra chickpea flour and toss the washed kale leaves in the chickpea flour.

Heat a small frying pan with the oil and bring it to 150°C (300°F). You can check it is at the right temperature with a thermometer or by placing a small spoonful of batter into the pan, if the oil is ready the kale will float and crisp up quite quickly. Set up a side plate lined with kitchen paper ready for the cooked kale.

Dip the dusted kale leaves in the chickpea batter, one by one and then very carefully place the leaves into the oil, cook each leaf alone, turning the kale carefully half-way through using a slotted spoon. The cooking time will vary depending on the kale, but each piece will take around 5 mintues to become golden and crispy. Carefully take the kale from the oil with the slotted spoon and place onto the kitchen paper to remove the excess oil. Repeat until you have cooked all of the kale.

Check the rice is cooked, by which time everything should be coming together. Serve each element in separate bowls as we have done here, or serve the hot rice on a plate, followed by the curry, the sizzling tempeh, the extra kimchi and the crispy kale. Finish with a spoonful of yoghurt, some coriander and a good squeeze of lime.

THE SPRING BOARD

Fermented Focaccia, Griddled
Asparagus, Red Radishes and
all the Trimmings

This spring celebration is filled with those fleeting ingredients
that you must make the most of when they are here! With grilled
asparagus and wild garlic pesto, these ingredients are here
to support you. They are also very portable and perfect for
picnics. I love eating this dish anytime from morning to night,
and exploring different flavour combinations. Enjoy it hot or
cold, changing the toppings with the seasons.

Serves: 4–5

Time taken: 1 hour,
   plus overnight fermentation

For the focaccia

350g (12oz) buckwheat flour
350ml (1½ cups) water, at room temperature
2 tbsp psyllium husk
80ml (⅓ cup) water, warm
1 tbsp dried active yeast
1 tbsp honey or rapadura sugar
150ml olive oil
1 sprig of rosemary, chopped
2 tbsp charcoal salt or regular salt

For the wild garlic pesto

100g (3½oz) hemp seeds
50g (1¾oz) wild garlic,
   washed and chopped
25g (generous ¼ cup) parsley,
   washed and chopped
4 tbsp nutritional yeast
½ tsp dried chilli flakes
1 tsp salt
100ml (⅓ cup) olive oil

For the asparagus

1 tbsp olive oil
Bunch of asparagus, washed and woody ends
   removed
¼ tsp salt

To serve

5 fresh radishes
Selection of pickles and ferments

Preheat the oven to 180°C fan (200°C/400°F/Gas 6).

FOCACCIA Whisk together the buckwheat flour and 300ml of the
room temperature water until smooth, and place into a covered glass
jar or bowl to ferment overnight. You will know it is ready when the
mixture is lightly aerated.

In a separate bowl, mix the psyllium husks with 50ml of the water and
leave to gel. In another bowl, add the warm water to the yeast and sugar
and leave it for 10 minutes to activate the yeast, you will see it coming
to life as a froth forms in the bowl.

In a large bowl mix the fermented mixture with the psyllium and yeast,
making sure everything is well combined. The mixing motion should be
more of a fold than a whisk so as to keep the bread light and airy.

Add the oil, chopped rosemary and salt and mix again, then leave the
bowl in a warm place covered with a damp cloth to rise for 1 hour. After
this time, knock back the dough on a floured surface and then place
onto a medium sized baking tray with high edges, lined with baking
paper and greased. Cover with a cloth once more to rise somewhere
warm for another hour, then bake for 40 minutes until crisp on top.

PESTO Meanwhile, make the wild garlic pesto. Place all of the
ingredients, apart from the olive oil, into a food processor and process
until well combined, ensuring that there are no large leaves left.
Gradually stream in the olive oil and taste for seasoning. Set aside until
ready to serve.

ASPARAGUS Heat a large griddle pan over a medium heat with the oil.
Place the asparagus spears into the hot pan and grill until they are soft
and charred. Turn off the heat and season them with salt.

Carefully cut the focaccia into pieces. Garnish a large board with
radishes and ferments and then top with the griddled asparagus and a
good drizzle of garlicky pesto.

RAINBOW FLATBREADS

Fibre is a really important part of our general health, especially when we are talking about our minds and guts. Fibre is found in so many plants and whole grains and helps us to digest food, keep things moving and support our bodies. These rainbow flatbreads are so versatile and such a great quick meal at any time of year. Once you have tried them, let your imagination go wild with different flavour combinations.

Serves: 4
Time taken: 30 minutes

400g (14oz) squash, chopped into small cubes
1 tbsp olive oil
100g (½ cup) cherry tomatoes, halved
¼ tsp salt
1 tsp smoked paprika
Large handful of leaves and/or sprouts, to serve
1 avocado, crumbled plant-based cheese
    or tahini sauce, to serve

For the salsa verde
150ml (⅔ cup) hemp or olive oil
30g (⅓ cup) parsley, finely chopped
1 garlic clove
1 tbsp red wine vinegar
1 tbsp Dijon mustard
2 tbsp capers, finely chopped
1 mint sprig
½ tsp salt

For the flatbreads
200g (7oz) buckwheat flour
225g (generous 1 cup) plant-based yoghurt
½ tsp baking powder
1 garlic clove, crushed
1 tbsp olive oil
½ tsp salt

Optional additions for the flatbreads
1 tbsp turmeric powder and
    ½ tsp chilli flakes (Lift)
2 tbsp beetroot juice (Balance)
1 tbsp hemp protein and 1 pipette CBD (Calm)

Preheat the oven to 180°C fan (200°C/400°F/Gas 6).

VEGETABLES Place the squash on a baking tray and drizzle with the olive oil and 1 tablespoon of water. Roast the squash for 10 minutes. Add the cherry tomatoes with the salt and smoked paprika. Shake everything around and then bake for another 15 minutes, shaking it every so often so that the squash is soft and crisp and everything else is cooked and gorgeously gooey.

SALSA VERDE Meanwhile, make the salsa verde by mixing all the ingredients together in a bowl. Set the dressing aside while everything else comes together.

FLATBREADS Add all of the ingredients to a large mixing bowl and knead the mixture with your hands until the dough comes together and easily rolls into a soft ball. Depending on your chosen plant-based yoghurt, you may need a little more or less flour, so that by the time the dough is mixed, it shouldn't be too sticky and should be easy to roll into a ball without cracking. If you decide to add an extra splash of colour, you may need a little more flour, especially if you use the beetroot.

On a floured surface, divide the dough into four equal parts and roll it into round flatbreads, each about 3mm (⅛in) thick. Keep the dough rotating and dust it with flour as you go, so that it doesn't stick to the floured surface.

Heat a large frying pan over a medium heat and add the flatbreads one by one. Cook each flatbread for 2 minutes on each side, so that they are lightly golden and cooked through.

If you are making a few flatbreads, place them on a baking tray in the oven while the other ingredients cook, making sure that they are in the oven for less than 5 minutes to avoid drying them out.

Serve the flatbreads laden with the roasted vegetables, scattered leaves and either avocado, crumbled cheese or tahini sauce. Finish with a drizzle of the vibrant salsa verde.

SWEET POTATO PASTA WITH WALNUT 'CHORIZO'

This sweet potato dish is a great mid-week meal. You can make the chorizo and serve it with any pasta at all. I love to use bean and quinoa pastas as a gluten-free alternative, and this sweet potato pasta is a great way to enjoy the benefits of bold and bright sweet potatoes in your day. The walnut 'chorizo' celebrates walnuts, a Mind Food star ingredient, this time spicy and savoury, packed full of flavour and giving great texture to this 'smoky' pasta dish, but can also be used in many ways in tacos, salads and as a topping to baked potato.

Serves: 2
Time taken: 45 minutes

1 sweet potato, washed, dried and
    spiralized or peeled into long
    thin ribbons
1 tbsp plant-based butter
1 garlic clove, crushed

For the walnut 'chorizo'
1 tbsp ground cumin
1 tbsp fennel seeds
200g (1½ cups) walnuts, soaked for at least
    1 hour and rinsed
100g (3½oz) carrots (about 1 medium),
    peeled and chopped
100g (scant 1 cup) sun-dried tomatoes,
    in oil (or soaked if dried)
50g (½ cup) black olives, pitted
2 tbsp maple syrup
1 tbsp brown miso
2 tbsp rosemary oil
2 tbsp smoked paprika

For the crispy capers
3 tbsp olive oil
3 tbsp capers, rinsed and patted dry

TIP – Capers have high concentrations of quercetin, a polyphenol that has been linked to decreased anxiety and depression.

Preheat the oven to 160°C fan (180°C/350°F/Gas 4). Line a small baking tray with baking paper.

WALNUT 'CHORIZO' Toast the cumin and fennel seeds in a small frying pan over a low heat for 1 minute until they are lightly toasted, to enhance their flavour.

Place the walnuts in a food processor or blender with the rest of the ingredients and the toasted spices and process into a crumb-like consistency, so there are no large pieces remaining.

Spread the walnut mixture onto the lined tray, about 1cm (½in) thick and fairly tightly packed – if the mixture is too spread out it will dry out too quickly. Bake for 30 minutes until it looks gooey and darker in colour.

CAPERS Heat the oil in a small frying pan over a medium–high heat until hot. Add the capers and cook for 3–4 minutes until crispy. Place the crispy capers on a piece of kitchen paper to absorb any excess oil.

Finally, make the sweet potato pasta. Fill a small saucepan with water and bring it to the boil with a pinch of salt. Add the sweet potato ribbons and cook for 1 minute until slightly soft, then drain the water.

Heat a frying pan over a medium heat with the butter and add the crushed garlic for 20 seconds, followed by the sweet potato pasta. Cook until coated in butter and hot but not too soft.

Turn the heat off the pasta and add a few tablespoons of the walnut 'chorizo'. Twirl the sweet potato pasta onto your plate and sprinkle with crispy capers. Enjoy with some plant-based parmesan if liked and extra 'chorizo'.

SMOKED CARROTS ON CHARCOAL PANCAKES

These carrots are a nod towards smoked salmon and such a creative way to recreate that uniquely smokey salty flavour in a plant-based way. There is something so exciting about working out how to reimagine anything just using good, honest in-season vegetables. It's a real showstopper for a weekend brunch with friends and a great meal if you decide to make a big batch and enjoy in several portions throughout the week, tossing the carrots through salads or cooking in stir-fries.

Serves: 4-6

Time taken: 2.5 hours,
 plus overnight fermentation

2 nori sheets
3 large carrots, peeled, topped and tailed
3 tbsp smoked salt
3 tbsp smoked paprika
2 whole star anise
½ cup kelp or dulse flakes
150–200ml (⅔-scant 1 cup) olive oil

To serve
1 batch of Cultured Pancake Batter
 (see page 169)
1 batch of Cultured Cashew Cream
 (see page 168)
Handful of Rosemary Walnuts
 (see page 153)
Handful of washed green leaves
1 lemon

TIP – These savoury pancakes can be made in so many flavour combinations. There are pancakes for any mood!

Preheat the oven to 180°C fan (200°C/400°F/Gas 6).

CARROTS Line a small baking tin with high sides with one sheet of foil and one sheet of baking paper – both pieces should be large enough that they will be able to seal the whole way around the carrots without any gap.

Place one nori sheet on the baking paper, then cut the peeled carrots in half and lay them onto the nori, squeezing each one next to the other as tightly as possible. You should be able to make two layers of carrots, depending on your topping.

Sprinkle the carrots with the salt, paprika, star anise and seaweed and then top with the other nori sheet. Drench the carrots in olive oil, making sure they are totally submerged. We are cooking them 'confit', meaning cooking under oil, which gives them a gloriously soft texture.

Seal the paper and foil around the carrots, scrunching the foil to make a tight seal and being careful not to leave any holes for the oil to escape. Bake for 2 hours until the carrots are soft. You can check them by very carefully opening the parcel and piercing a knife the whole way through a carrot to check it is soft. Leave the carrots to cool. When they reach room temperature, pour the oil into a jar to use for dressings.

Place the cooked carrots on your chopping board, soft side down, and finely slice horizontally, making long thin slices. This simple and meditative way in which you carefully slice the carrots once they are cooked is the key to making them resemble smoked salmon.

PANCAKES Heat a frying pan over a medium heat with a little oil and ladle the pancake batter into the pan to make rounds the size of a coaster. Cook them for 1 minute on each side and continue until you have the number of pancakes you would like.

Top each pancake with some Cultured Cashew Cream, the smoked carrots, Rosemary Walnuts and leaves, dressing each pancake with a drizzle of the cooking oil and a squeeze of lemon.

LIFT
Kimchi, avocado
and bee pollen

BALANCE
Carrot lox and
sourcream

SOOTHE
Black beans, harissa
and leaves

FOCUS
Grilled lion's mane, sour
cream and massaged kale

CHILL
CBD slaw and
toasted seeds

SUMMER

Summer is a time of release, change and beginnings. This time of year does so much more than just clearing our heads, pulling us outdoors for a change of scene with the sun having the power to enhance our mood and energy.

Many of us relate the summer time to festivals, filled with long days in a field, rain or shine. A time of letting go, going a little bit wild and shaking things up. To me, festivals totally sum up what the summer really means to most people – a time to be spontaneous, creative, free, hot and sociable.

Mind Food more than anything is about connecting both yourself and others through food. These dishes are inspired by that fun summer feeling; they spark conversations and are a little bit more interactive than the other three seasons – a laugh while that familiar corn butter dribbles down our chin or a smile when we bite into that first sweet strawberry. I hope these bright, bold and carefree flavours take you back to your own particular sunny place, wherever it may be.

INGREDIENTS FOR SUMMER

QUIETING THE MIND

Meditation is becoming more and more widely understood, but there is still a common belief that it is hard to do. The idea of sitting quietly alone for a period of time can be enough to put some people off, so try exploring different meditations that might work for you. There are apps like Headspace and Insight Timer that offer versatile and personalized tools for learning to meditate. There are also ancient practices like Vedic meditation that can be extremely useful.

To me, cooking is a moving mediation, as walking and dance can be, when your mind is somewhere away from your thoughts and you are relaxed yet focused on a task. This can be just as powerful as other forms of meditation. Don't be fooled by your preconceptions, break out of repeptitive thoughts and know there is a practice out there to suit you.

QI GONG

Qi Gong is a type of ancient movement, which began in China. *Qi*, pronounced 'chi', and *Gong* together mean 'life-force practice'. This incredible ancient art is a form of movement that can support and strengthen our own energy and can be done in a routine or as a few moves that support a specific need.

You can find Qi Gong classes and routines online or in person in many places around the world and adopting a few simple moves as part of your own morning routine can be hugely beneficial. A Qi Gong routine often begins with lightly tapping the body and shaking, so if nothing else, you could try following a short practice to start your day. It is a gentle yet uplifting practice that will help you move and shift your mindset.

BREATHWORK

This is a practice that I have found hugely transformative over the years. The first time I tried it, I was amazed at what emerged, what was released and how I felt afterwards. Breathwork is a practice that uses the breath in different ways and there are many different styles to explore.

"Breathing is the easiest and most instrumental part of the autonomic nervous system to control and navigate. In fact, the way you breathe strongly affects the chemical and physiological activities in your body"

—Wim Hoff

Breathwork comes in many styles, so it can be useful to connect with different practitioners and find one that suits you. This practice is particularly helpful for reducing symptoms associated with anxiety, depression, insomnia and PTSD. Breathwork must be done in a supported environment, particularly if you are trying it for the first time, as it can bring up challenging emotions. There are benefits even just to being more aware of your breath and moving away from shallow breathing, so just breathe!

ASTROLOGY

Astrology has been used for millennia to help people to better understand the movements of the planets and celestial bodies, and their influence on human affairs in the natural world. I have seen over the years the peace of mind that astrology can provide. By better understanding ourselves, we can make sense, not just of ourselves, but of those around us. Astrology is far more than just your zodiac sign, and finding out more about your birth chart can be a great place to start, to understand certain times in your life. If astrology isn't for you, look up numerology or human design to further understand who you are. Admittedly, this may not be for everyone, but I think in the future it will become more recognized as a way of understanding ourselves and our world.

SUMMER STRAWBERRY FOOL

This is a Mind Food take on a classic summer dessert, the strawberry fool. In this recipe, re-imagined as breakfast, the first of the summer strawberries are enrobed in cool hemp 'chocolate', hemp yoghurt and a nutty pistachio crunch. Whether you eat it for breakfast, dessert or an afternoon snack, these strawberries are here to bring a smile to your face and hopefully several moments of peace to your day.

Serves: 4
Time taken: 20 minutes

1 punnet of strawberries, washed
6–8 tbsp Hemp Yoghurt (see page 171)
    or coconut yoghurt
1 tbsp hemp seeds
1 tbsp pistachio nuts, shelled and
    roughly chopped

For the hemp 'chocolate'
50g (1¾oz) hemp seeds, plus extra for
    sprinkling (or desiccated coconut)
100ml (⅓ cup) Hemp Milk (see page 171)
Pinch of salt
20g (¾oz) agave
¼ tsp vanilla powder/extract
60g (2oz) coconut butter, melted
5 drops (250mg) CBD oil

Place half of the strawberries in the fridge with the tops intact. Chop the remaining strawberries, remove the tops and set aside.

HEMP 'CHOCOLATE' Make the hemp 'chocolate' by blending the hemp seeds and milk, salt, agave and vanilla in a high-speed blender. Once smooth, add the melted coconut butter and CBD oil, then blend again until silky. Pour into a small bowl ready for dipping.

STRAWBERRIES Line a plate with baking paper and take the strawberries out of the fridge. Dip each strawberry, one by one, into the hemp 'chocolate' and tap off any excess. Place on the baking paper and continue until all the strawberries are dipped.

Sprinkle over some hemp seeds or desiccated coconut for added texture, then place back in the fridge to set, which should only take a few moments.

Place the yoghurt in the bowls, followed by the chopped strawberries, hemp seeds and pistachio nuts, and finish with a hemp 'chocolate' strawberry, then just sit back and enjoy the sunshine.

BEYOND PEACHES AND CREAM CHIA

Chia seeds are known for their omega-3 benefits, a key part of brain health, and also for their warrior strength. Here, the mix of chia with oats and macadamia is a super creamy combination, made even better by the soft caramelized peaches and toasted coconut, for that all important crunch. Prepare this breakfast the night before you want it, as the chia seeds need to soak up the liquid in order to be ready.

Serves: 4
Time taken: 12 hours

100g (¾ cup) macadamia nuts, soaked for
    at least 8 hours and rinsed
30g (⅔ cup) chia seeds
¼ tsp vanilla extract or 1 tonka bean, grated
2 tbsp honey
½ tsp salt

For the peaches
2 ripe peaches, halved and stoned
½ tsp rapadura or coconut sugar
1 tsp chopped fresh rosemary

To serve
50g (1¾oz) macadamia nuts, chopped
4 tbsp Hemp Yoghurt (see page 171)
    or coconut yoghurt

CHIA Blend the macadamia nuts with 300ml of water for at least 1 minute, until smooth.

Pour the macadamia milk into a large glass jar, then add the chia seeds, vanilla, honey and salt, whisking with a fork to combine. Transfer to the fridge for at least 4 hours or overnight.

PEACHES Sprinkle the peach halves with the sugar and the rosemary, then either grill or griddle the peaches until caramelized. This will take 5–10 minutes depending on the ripeness of the peaches.

Serve the caramelized peach halves on top of the chia with a spoonful of Hemp Yoghurt. Sprinkle with the macadamia nuts, roughly chopped.

TIP – You can serve this dish cold for 3 days after it is first made, so prep ahead, then try using the peaches with your overnight oats, porridge or even as a light summer pudding.

CHICKPEA AND BLUSHED TOMATO TART

This tart full of vibrant colour is an incredible addition to the summer table, especially when you have a crisp buttery pastry case, packed full of seasonal vegetables and enrobed in a creamy sauce. Making breadcrumbs is a totally cathartic experience when in the right headspace; I like to put on my favourite songs and sing along while I create this dish. A better headspace will make the flavours taste even better.

Serves: 6
Time taken: 1 hour

For the tomato oil
10 cherry tomatoes, halved
1 garlic clove
100ml (scant ½ cup) olive oil
½ tsp salt
½ tsp smoked paprika
¼ tsp chilli flakes

For the chickpea pastry
200g (7oz) chickpea flour
200g (7oz) tapioca flour
100g (3½oz) cold plant-based butter
60ml (¼ cup) cold water
½ tsp smoked salt

For the cashew béchamel
150g (1¼ cups) soaked and rinsed cashews
450ml (scant 2 cups) filtered water
30ml (2 tbsp) olive oil
60g (2oz) chickpea flour
2 tbsp Dijon mustard
1 tbsp nutritional yeast
½ tsp salt

To serve
65g (1 cup) mixed salad leaves
30g (¼ cup) pecan nuts or
   pumpkin seeds, chopped
2 tbsp chopped chives
Sea salt and freshly cracked pepper

Preheat the oven to 180°C fan (200°C/400°F/Gas 6).

TOMATO OIL Roast the tomatoes and garlic, drizzled with half the olive oil and salt in a baking tray for 30 minutes until nicely blushed.

CHICKPEA PASTRY Add the flours to a large bowl with the butter and rub together lightly between your fingertips until it resembles breadcrumbs. Add the water and salt and continue mixing to bring the pastry together to form a dough. Be gentle with this pastry and do not over work it. Grease a 20cm tart tin, or three smaller tart tins, with a little of the butter or olive oil. Then, once a dough is formed, roll it out and carefully place into your greased tart tin or tins. You make need to patch up any cracks in the pastry, but it is quite easy to work with. Bake in the oven with the tomatoes for 10 minutes until golden.

When you remove the pastry from the oven, also check the garlic cloves in the tomato baking tray are soft, then take them from the oven, leaving the tomatoes inside.

CASHEW BÉCHAMEL Blend the cashews and water together until really smooth and then set aside. Heat the oil in a medium saucepan, add the chickpea flour and mix well with a wooden spoon. Gradually add the blended cashew milk, constantly stirring as you go, making sure there are no lumps. The mixture should thicken quickly. Add the mustard, nutritional yeast and salt and stir through. Pour this creamy mixture into the baked pastry case, making sure that the filling is even and smooth. Leave the tart to cool and then transfer it to the fridge to set.

When the tomatoes are caramelized, remove them from the oven to cool slightly and then transfer the tomatoes with their tomatoey oil to a blender with the remaining tomato oil ingredients. Blend thoroughly until the mixture goes bright red and there are no pieces.

Dress the salad leaves with a couple of spoonfuls of the cashew béchamel. Once the tart is set, serve it cool or warmed through for 10 minutes in the oven. Serve garnished with salad leaves, some nuts or seeds, chopped chives, salt and pepper and a splash of tomato oil.

SMASHING SUMMER SALAD

This mind-boosting salad recipe is perfect for long summer days, with a bold and bright selection of vegetables – green peas, red blushed tomatoes, golden potato crackling and dark leafy greens. Savour the contrast of hot potatoes with cool, sweet and salty vegetables and the soft, creamy and crispy textures in this plate. I hope this dish lives up to its name and helps to lift your spirits ready for a mellow summer in the sun.

Serves: 4
Time taken: 45 minutes

200g (7oz) new potatoes
60ml (¼ cup) olive oil
Handful of fresh tomatoes, halved
2 garlic cloves, skin on

For the smashed peas
200g (1⅓ cups) cooked peas
20g (¾oz) mint leaves,
    picked from the stalks
20g (¾oz) parsley leaves,
    picked from the stalks
Juice and zest of 1 lemon
1 tsp salt

To serve
1 avocado, stoned, peeled and finely sliced
100g (1½ cups) mixed salad leaves, washed
100ml (scant ½ cup) Maca and Mustard
    Dressing (see page 174)

TIP – To be especially prepared, you can make the peas and even par-boil the potatoes in large batches ahead of time and then reap the rewards by finishing off the hot crunchy potatoes when you are ready to feast.

Preheat the oven to 180°C fan (200°C/400°F/Gas 6) and line two baking trays with baking paper.

Clean your potatoes and cut them into quarters, across the middle, then in half again. Place the potatoes in a saucepan covered in water and bring to the boil. Leave to simmer for 20 minutes until cooked through, then drain through a colander, shaking as they drain to rough up the edges of the potatoes on the holes. Leave the potatoes to cool slightly and then sprinkle them with a pinch of salt.

Heat one of the lined baking trays with all but 2 tablespoons of the oil in the oven. Once it is hot, carefully tumble in the potatoes and place them back in the oven for 40 minutes, gently shaking the tray every 15 minutes to make sure the potatoes are golden and crunchy on all sides.

Meanwhile, toss the tomatoes with 1 tablespoon of the olive oil and a pinch of salt, then toss these tomatoes onto the other baking tray. Place the garlic cloves in their skins on the tray with the tomatoes, then roast for 20 minutes (with the potatoes still in the oven) until the tomatoes have lightly blushed and the garlic is soft, which enhances the flavour of these lovely summer tomatoes and changes their texture. Remove from the oven and leave to cool.

SMASHED PEAS Prepare the peas while the potatoes finish cooking. Add the peas to a food processor with the peeled, cooked garlic, herbs and half of the lemon zest and juice. Roughly mix and chop all of the ingredients together in the food processor. Whisk the remaining olive oil, lemon and salt together, set aside, then check the potatoes are ready to be removed from the oven.

To serve, place the peas and roasted tomatoes on plates, then add the crunchy potatoes, followed by some freshly cut buttery avocado, mixed salad leaves and a spiral of zingy dressing.

GARDEN OF MY MIND

This is a vibrant, fresh plate of seasonal goodness that always packs lots of flavour – raw courgettes, filled with a tangy lemon 'cheese' and garlicky chickpeas, finished with this especially flavoursome romesco sauce. Plus, it is my favourite dish ever to plate. A key part of Mind Food is doing that little bit extra just for you. Rather than just gathering everything on a plate, take a moment, meditate on it while rolling the courgettes, spreading the bright red sauce, scattering those bouncy chickpeas, then sprinkling greens over for the final touch.

Serves: 4
Time taken: 45 minutes

2 courgettes (zucchinis), washed
400g (2½ cups) chickpeas, cooked and
    drained (or 1 × 400g (14oz) tin, drained
    and rinsed)
Pinch of salt
1 garlic clove, crushed

For the romesco sauce
1 red pepper
30g (¼ cup) sun-dried tomatoes
60ml (¼ cup) sherry vinegar
150g (⅔ cup) almond butter
½ tsp dried chilli flakes
Salt and freshly cracked black pepper
180ml (¾ cup) olive oil

For the cashew cheese
5 tbsp Cultured Cashew Cream (see page 168)
Zest and juice of 1 lemon
1 tbsp nutritional yeast
Pinch of salt

To serve
Handful of cherry tomatoes
20g (⅓ cup) mixed salad leaves
50g (scant ½ cup) cashews, toasted
    and chopped

Preheat the oven to 180°C fan (200°C/400°F/Gas 6).

ROMESCO SAUCE Place the red pepper whole on a tray and bake for 30 minutes until soft and roasted, then remove from the oven and leave to cool before handling. Once cool, gently pull the stem from the flesh and the seeds should easily come out with it. Check inside for any remaining seeds and remove them.

Place the pepper with the remaining sauce ingredients, except the oil, into a food processor or blender. Process until well combined and then stream in the oil gradually. Season to taste then transfer the sauce to a container in the fridge to chill slightly before serving.

COURGETTES Top and tail the courgettes and use a peeler to carefully turn the courgettes into long ribbons, as wide as possible. Place the ribbons in a large bowl and sprinkle over a little salt and oil, then toss to evenly coat, which will slightly soften the courgettes, and set aside.

Finely chop the remaining centres of the courgettes. Heat a frying pan with a splash of oil and add the courgette offcuts and chickpeas with a pinch of salt. Sauté for a couple of minutes, then add the crushed garlic and cook for a further minute. Turn off the heat and set aside.

CASHEW CHEESE Mix the Cultured Cashew Cream with the lemon juice and zest, nutritional yeast and salt, then taste to check that it is to your liking. This will be the courgette filling.

Take the strips of courgette and lay three per person on a chopping board. Place one tablespoon of the cashew cheese at one end and roll the courgette around the filling until fully rolled.

To serve, place a spoonful of romesco sauce on a plate with the courgette rolls, fresh tomatoes and chickpea mixture. Top with salad leaves and toasted nuts, as well as a good pinch of salt and freshly cracked black pepper.

KIMCHI AND BLACK BEAN TOSTADAS

When I first started travelling in order to expand my knowledge of food, I went to America and was particularly impressed by the South American influences. Tamales, tostadas and quesadillas were new words to me and I was excited to explore what was possible; I was blown away by their high energy and lively flavours. This energy is totally in line with the Mind Food ethos. Here, I wanted to do a take on tostadas with brain-boosting black beans, a tangy dressing laced with pomegranate and CBD, all with a crunchy kimchi base.

Makes: 20 tostadas

Time taken: 30 minutes,
    plus overnight fermentation (optional)

For the tostadas

100g (3½oz) chickpea flour
100ml (scant ½ cup) Clever Kimchi
    (see page 161), or store-bought kimchi,
    finely chopped and drained
150g (5½oz) buckwheat flour
100ml (scant ½ cup) olive oil

For the CBD slaw

2 cups grated roots, such as parsnips or carrots
1 batch Pomegranate and CBD Dressing
    (see page 177)

For the black beans

1 × 400g (14oz) tin of black beans
Zest and juice of 1 lime
¼ tsp salt
1 avocado, halved, stoned and flesh cubed
20g (¾oz) coriander, chopped

For the buttered corn

1 tbsp plant-based butter
50g (⅓ cup) sweetcorn kernels,
    fresh or frozen
¼ tsp salt
¼ tsp chilli flakes

To serve

Sprouts or leaves, to garnish

TOSTADAS In a glass bowl, whisk together the chickpea flour with 50ml (scant ¼ cup) of water until smooth and leave to ferment overnight. This step is not essential, but makes the batter more exciting.

CBD SLAW Pour the dressing over the grated roots and set aside to marinate while you prepare the rest of the dish.

BLACK BEANS Drain the black beans, then place them in a bowl with the lime juice, zest and salt and stir. Then add the avocado and coriander and lightly crush everything with a fork.

TOSTADAS When the chickpea batter is fermented, fold in the kimchi, without the brine, and add the buckwheat flour. The buckwheat flour will bind the dough together into a firmer dough that is easy to roll out and work with. If the dough is sticky add more buckwheat flour until you have something the consistency of pastry dough.

Flour a clean work surface and roll the dough out to 2mm (⅛in) thick and then use a pastry cutter to create 7–10cm (3–4in) rounds. Repeat until you have the number of tostadas you need. The remaining dough can be kept in a sealed container in the fridge.

Heat a large frying pan with half of the olive oil and add the rolled tostadas, making sure to spread it into little round pancake shapes. Fry for 2–3 minutes on each side until golden, then repeat with the batter and oil until the batter is used up.

BUTTERED CORN Heat a small frying pan and melt the butter. Add the corn and fry with the salt and chilli until golden – about 3–4 minutes. Remove from the heat and prepare to serve.

Once cooked, place the crispy tostadas onto your plate and top with black beans, buttered corn and CBD slaw, then finish with a squeeze of lime and some sprouts or leaves to garnish.

HARISSA TAMALES AND BUTTERED CORN

I first discovered tamales while training in New York and I recall asking my teacher at the time to name his favourite thing to make – the answer was tamales. Tamales are dishes from South America and are an incredible street food made from corn masa (flour). I think of them as South American 'pasties' and there are so many different filling options. The dough itself is soft and sweet and the filling can be anything from spicy beans to roasted vegetables to this less traditional tamale filled with a hemp pesto.

Serves: 4
Time taken: 1 hour

For the harissa
1 red pepper, deseeded and chopped
200ml (scant 1 cup) olive oil
   (or split coconut)
2 tbsp smoked paprika
Zest and juice of 1 lemon
¼ tsp dried chilli flakes
½ tsp sweet paprika
¼ tsp salt

For the tamales
200ml (scant 1 cup) vegetable stock
   or water
200g (7oz) masa harina
1 tsp salt
50ml (scant ¼ cup) olive oil
8 chard leaves or corn husks
1 batch of Hemp and Parsley Pesto
   (see page 175)

For the buttered corn
1 × 400ml (14fl oz) coconut milk
1 corn-on-the-cob, kernels removed,
   or 200g (1½ cups) corn kernels,
   frozen or fresh
¼ tsp drilled chilli flakes
Zest of 1 lemon

TIP – Traditionally, tamales are made in huge batches, then heated up through the week or taken as an on-the-go lunch.

Preheat the oven to 180°C fan (200°C/400°F/Gas 6).

HARISSA First, make the harissa. Place the pepper on a roasting tray, with a splash of the oil, then roast for 15 minutes until soft. Remove the pepper from the oven and transfer to a food processor or blender and blend with the rest of the harissa ingredients until smooth. Set aside or place in a jar in the fridge.

TAMALES Next, make the tamales. Warm the stock through in a saucepan until simmering, but not boiling, or boil the kettle if using just water. Add the masa harina and salt to a food processor or blender, then stream in the warm liquid while the processor is on. The flour will start to absorb the liquid and the dough will start to form.

Add the oil and 4 tablespoons of the harissa sauce, then process again, making sure everything is well mixed through. The dough should form into a soft ball when rolled, at which time it shouldn't crack, but also shouldn't be too wet. When the dough is the correct consistency, leave it to sit for 10 minutes to firm up slightly.

Lay the chard leaves or corn husks flat on a chopping board ready to make the tamales. Add around 100g (3½oz) of the dough and flatten the dough into neat rectangles about 5mm (¼in) thick – the exact size will depend on your chosen leaves or husks.

Add around 1 tablespoon of Hemp and Parsley Pesto along the bottom third of the tamale in a neat line. Fold the top of the tamale over the bottom, sealing the edges and neatening the sides of the dough so that the pesto is totally enclosed. Fold the leaf or husk around the edge, folding in the sides like a parcel so that the dough is also totally enclosed.

When the tamales are ready, set up a large saucepan of boiling water with a steamer and place the tamales inside the steamer with the lid on. Steam over a medium heat for 20–30 minutes and then remove and let them sit for 5 minutes, as the tamales will firm up once cool. Serve whole on a plate if using chard, or unwrapped if using corn husks.

BUTTERED CORN While the tamales cook, make the buttered corn. Heat the coconut milk in a saucepan over a high heat for up to 5 minutes, until the milk splits. Season it well with plenty of salt and separate the solid coconut butter from the oil.

Place the corn kernels in a saucepan over a high heat with a tablespoon of the coconut butter and sizzle until golden. Add the chilli flakes and grate loads of lemon zest over the corn and stir through.

Serve the tamales on a plate, while still warm, with a splash of harissa and the buttered corn.

A MEZZE OF THE MIND

Pistachio Falafel, Cauliflower
Couscous and Beetroot Tahini

This mezze brings me back to a good summer festival in Glastonbury, where we used to hike up to the Healing Fields to this incredible and quirky falafel café. Rain or shine, my friends and I would be there, totally exhausted from days in the Fields, covered in glitter and wearing the customary soggy wellies. Falafels always provide perfect comfort especially when served with loads of sauce. This *Mind Food* version is packed full of colours and flavours, perfect to enjoy through the week, or for a feast for you and your friends.

Serves: 4
Time taken: 1 hour

For the pistachio falafel
100g (scant ¾ cup) shelled pistachios
400g (2½ cups) chickpeas, cooked and
  drained (or 1 × 400g (14oz) tin, drained
  and rinsed)
30g (⅓ cup) parsley
150g (2½ cups) broccoli florets
1 garlic clove
½ tsp ground coriander
½ tsp dried chilli flakes
¼ tsp salt
2 tbsp chickpea flour, plus extra for rolling
Olive oil, as needed

For the beetroot tahini
1 medium beetroot, peeled and
  chopped into smaller pieces
200g (scant 1 cup) tahini
100ml (⅓ cup) water
50ml (scant ¼ cup) olive oil
1 garlic clove, roasted
½ tsp salt

For the cauliflower couscous
1 cauliflower, washed, dried and cut into
  smaller pieces, leaves and all
20g (¾oz) parsley, plus extra to serve
20g (¾oz) coriander, plus extra to serve
10g (½oz) mint, plus extra to serve
2 tbsp olive oil
1 lemon

1 pomegranate, deseeded, to serve

First preheat your oven to 170°C fan (190°C/375°F/Gas 5).

FALAFEL Place all of the falafel ingredients in a food processor or blender and process to combine, adding a little olive oil as necessary, so you have a thick but smooth paste with no large pieces. This dough should roll easily into a ball – if it's too crumbly, add more olive oil and if it's too wet and sticky, add a little more flour.

Place a few tablespoons of chickpea flour on a plate and add a pinch of salt. Roll the blended mixture into round falafels the size of an avocado stone and then toss each one in the flour. Squash each one into more of a disk shape and place them onto a baking tray.

Generously drizzle the falafels with olive oil and bake for 25 minutes until golden, turning each one half way through cooking, so they are crisp and golden on all sides.

TAHINI For the beetroot tahini, place all of the ingredients into a food processor or blender and blend until super smooth. Taste to ensure that it's seasoned as you like. Transfer to a container and store in the fridge until ready to serve.

COUSCOUS For the cauliflower couscous, place all of the ingredients into a food processor or blender and process until you have a consistency like couscous and not too over-processed.

To serve, place the beetroot tahini on the plate – splash it if you dare by lightly tapping the plate with the back of your spoon; this may take a little bit of practise, so be prepared, as it may make a mess first time. Make a bed of cauliflower couscous and lay three falafels on each plate sprinkled with the pomegranate seeds and extra herbs. You could also just allow everyone to share from a serving platter. Enjoy the falafels warm or pack them up for a great packed lunch.

AUTUMN

In a time when we are settling in for darker days, many are affected by the change of seasons. We often associate autumn with that back-to-school feeling and that urge to reorganize ourselves and put a plan in place often emerges. As the days become darker, the sometimes dramatic effect this can have on our moods is widely recognized. If you feel this shift in your life, perhaps it's time to explore ways to shed a little light on the season, literally.

Through food, this can mean eating brighter, bolder vegetables and ingredients that naturally contain vitamin D, like spinach and kale. Also, try and get outside in the fresh air to get some sunlight, even if it's not so warm, and bring some gentle heat to your bones through movement.

To me, autumn tastes very much as it looks, full of deep rich colours, warm sunsets and the last flavours of the summer. So, as we prepare ourselves for a different pace, this is the time to tuck into warmer foods with a sprinkle of the preserved summer harvest. This is a time of year where nourishment is key to keeping our immunity strong and energy up as the light fades.

INGREDIENTS FOR AUTUMN

KUNDALINI YOGA

Kundalini is a combination of often repetitive movement, breath techniques, sound and meditation and can seem a little far out on your first experience of it. It is said that kundalini was kept secret until it was first brought to the west by Yogi Bajan and is now taught around the world.

Known to be especially useful for those experiencing addiction and stuck patterning, it derives from the Sanskrit word *kundal*, meaning 'coiled energy', and works by moving the energy up from the base of the spine, through the chakras and up to the head.

Kundalini yoga is my favourite yoga practice and I find its wild movements and unique practices somewhat shifting and moving. The benefits are endless and unique, but can be anything from building strength and improving flexibility to supporting your digestion, immunity and mental clarity.

ACUPUNCTURE

Acupuncture is the alternative therapy that helped me to shift my own disordered eating. After years with a good therapist, she went away for a few weeks and encouraged me to try acupuncture, which involves using needles in particular points through the body. Originally sceptical, this was the first time I saw results and one of the first times I had tried any ancient practices. After a few months of weekly treatments something shifted emotionally and I felt like I wanted to get better, whereas before I did not.

Acupuncture is derived from Chinese medicine and works by stimulating points linked to organs or energy channels in the body that might be causing issues. An acupuncture session involves a consultation with a practitioner and then lying down while they insert tiny needles that make a small but mostly pain-free sensation. The needles remain in place for a short while, then are removed before you take it easy for the rest of the day.

I learned from trying it that there may be huge benefits from being open to different ideas and therapies. All is not lost when you feel stuck: there's always a way through, just maybe not the way you would think.

AYURVEDA

Ayurveda is the traditional Hindu system of medicine (incorporated in Atharva Veda, the last of the four Vedas) which is based on the idea of balance in bodily systems and uses diet, herbal treatment and yogic breathing.

Ayurveda defines three body types and uses them to work out the best natural ways to bring the individual back into balance, and remedies are diet and lifestyle related.

Ayurveda can be helpful for our mental health as sometimes metal health issues are triggered or accentuated by a bodily symptom. When more traditional medicine is not getting to the root of the issue, exploring different routes can be nominally beneficial and if you are only slightly off-balance in some way or looking to learn more about yourself, Ayurveda can be a hugely beneficial and fascinating support system.

WILD RASPBERRY WAFFLES WITH HEMP YOGHURT AND CANDIED SEEDS

Waffles are known as a more indulgent meal and this version is no different, nurturing sweet waffle memories in a totally *Mind Food* way. These are Belgium-style waffles that are crisp, fluffy and slightly smaller than their American equivalents. This particular batter is fermented so start the preparation the day before you want to have them and consider preparing a double batch of the pre-ferment to use in other recipes or to make more waffles through the week.

Serves: 4

Time taken: 40 minutes,
   plus overnight fermentation

140g (5oz) buckwheat flour
125ml (½ cup) Hemp Milk (see page 171)
½ tbsp brown rice vinegar
20g (¾oz) plant-based butter or coconut
   oil, plus extra for greasing
2 tbsp maple syrup
Large pinch of salt
¼ tsp baking powder
30g (scant ⅓ cup) almond flour

For the candied seeds
50g (⅓ cup) pumpkin seeds
1 tbsp maple syrup
¼ tsp salt

For the wild raspberry relish
1 tbsp olive oil
2.5cm (1in) piece of fresh ginger,
   chopped into thin matchsticks
200g (1⅓ cups) frozen raspberries
2 tbsp honey or maple syrup
½ lemon

For the rose syrup
200ml (6¾ fl oz) honey or agave
1 tsp rose water

To serve
2 tbsp Hemp Yoghurt (see page 171)
   or coconut yoghurt

Pre-ferment 50g (1¾oz) of the buckwheat flour with 50ml (scant ¼ cup) of water by mixing them together, ensuring there are no lumps. Decant the mixture into a glass jar and leave the jar lightly covered at room temperature for 24 hours to ferment. During this time, prepare your toppings ready for the moment of truth.

CANDIED SEEDS To make the candied seeds, place a small saucepan over a medium heat. Add the seeds to the pan and toast them until they start to pop and then add some olive oil, followed by the maple syrup. The maple syrup will lightly caramelize over the seeds and any liquid will evaporate. Turn off the heat at this point and add a pinch of salt. Set the pumpkin seeds aside to cool and then place them in a jar until you are ready to use them.

RASPBERRY RELISH To make the wild raspberry relish, first heat the olive oil in a small saucepan over a medium heat until warm. Add the ginger, lightly frying it to release the aroma. Add the raspberries and honey and cook the mixture down until it resembles jam. At this point, turn off the heat and add a few gratings of lemon zest and a squeeze of lemon juice, roughly 1 tablespoon of each. Leave to cool and place the jam in a jar and leave in the fridge until you are ready to use it.

ROSE SYRUP To make the rose syrup, mix the honey or agave with the rose water and store in a small jar until ready to use.

WAFFLES The next day, combine the Hemp Milk and brown rice vinegar and leave to sit for 5 minutes.

Melt the butter or coconut oil and once they are melted, add them to a heatproof bowl with the hemp milk mixture, the fermented buckwheat and the maple syrup.

Sieve the salt, baking powder and almond flour into the same bowl and stir everything together thoroughly. The waffle batter at this point should be the consistency of regular pancake batter, which is nicely pourable like double (heavy) cream. Leave the batter to rest for 5–10 minutes before cooking.

Heat the waffle iron until smoking hot and once it is heated, paint the griddles with a little extra coconut oil. Ladle the batter into each iron and cook for 6 minutes until the outsides are crispy. Timings might vary depending on your machine, but when you see that the steam stops coming from the edges, you will know that they are ready.

Carefully open the iron and remove the waffles, which should crisp more as soon as they are removed from the waffle iron. Place them on serving plates to crisp while you gather together the fillings. Top with the wild raspberry relish, candied seeds, rose water syrup and Hemp Yoghurt to serve.

TIP – If you don't have a waffle iron, you can make this into pancakes with exactly the same base recipe.

OAT FRITTERS, WINDFALL APPLE SLAW AND CANDIED WALNUTS

These oat fritters are a great breakfast or lunch dish. Oats are naturally soothing and substantial and so they make a great meal to keep you going through the day. These could be made sweet or savoury and are inspired by a sweet recipe taught in one of my cookery classes by the chef Arthur Potts-Dawson.

Make the batter ahead of time and make these fritters for a few days in a row, perhaps trying different flavour combinations each time.

Serves: 2
Time taken: 30 minutes

175g (scant 2 cups) gluten-free oats or
  millet flakes
3 tsp baking powder
½ tsp bicarbonate of soda (baking soda)
275ml (generous 1 cup) oat milk
1 tbsp apple cider vinegar
Olive oil, for frying

For the apple slaw
2 pieces of kale, washed
½ tsp sea salt
4 tbsp olive oil
1 tbsp apple cider vinegar
1 tbsp Dijon mustard
½ tsp honey
1 large apple, cut into matchsticks
30g (⅓ cup) parsley, finely chopped
200g (7oz) celeriac, peeled and grated
50g (¼ cup) Rosemary Walnuts
  (see page 153)

To serve
3–4 tbsp Sprouted Chickpea Hummus
  (see page 176)

OAT FRITTERS Put the oats in a food processor or blender and blend into a 'flour'. Transfer the 'flour' to a bowl, mix in the baking powder and bicarbonate of soda and then add the oat milk and apple cider vinegar. Mix until well combined.

APPLE SLAW To make the apple slaw, strip the kale from the stems, break the leaves into small pieces and finely chop the stems. Rub the kale with a little of the salt and oil, then add to a large bowl.

Add the rest of the oil, apple cider vinegar, mustard and honey and mix well. Add the apple, parsley and celeriac and toss to combine, finishing with the remaining salt. Crumble over the Rosemary Walnuts and set to one side.

Heat a frying pan with a little olive oil and ladle in some of the pancake batter, spreading the mixture into rounds. Cook over a medium heat for a few minutes until you see little bubbles appear. Flip over and cook each fritter for another 3 minutes, until golden brown on both sides.

Add a couple of fritters to each plate, top with Sprouted Chickpea Hummus and then the apple slaw. Enjoy warm, then just relax.

TIP – In Mind Food, we love garlicky green fritters for that extra dose of greens, but if you're looking for more grounding or comfort you can try adding a handful of grated carrots with ½ teaspoon of turmeric and chilli flakes for an even more warming experience.

MISO PORRIDGE

I love a savoury breakfast, especially at times when I am feeling slightly anxious. This particular recipe I find very grounding and satisfying, especially as the seasons change. Mind Food is all about breaking convention and understanding your individual needs, for example tuning into when you like to eat in the morning. Personally, I mix things up, sometimes eating within the first hour of being awake and some days I love to work out first and then have a slightly heartier meal later, at which time this porridge perfectly fits perfectly.

Serves: 2

Time taken: 20 minutes

2 tbsp olive oil

150g (scant 1 cup) brown rice flakes or gluten-free oats

600ml (2½ cups) vegetable stock or water

2 tbsp dark miso

1 tbsp peanut butter

1 tsp lion's mane mushroom powder (optional)

To serve

½ cup Massaged Kale (see page 178) or washed leaves

3 tbsp peanuts, toasted

½ tsp dried chilli flakes

½ avocado, peeled, stoned and chopped (optional)

2 tbsp Hot Sauce (see page 174)

Heat a medium-sized saucepan on a medium heat and add the rice flakes or oats to toast for two minutes. Next, add the stock and cook for five minutes until the oats are the consistency you would like them.

Add the miso, peanut butter and lion's mane powder, if using, and stir thoroughly through the oats.

Transfer to a bowl and garnish with a handful of Massaged Kale or leaves and a sprinkle of peanuts, chilli flakes, avocado and the Hot Sauce. Enjoy hot, which will enable you to positively embrace the day ahead.

TIP – Kale is an ingredient I have leaned on since discovering Mind Food. It's an easy way to add a portion of leafy greens to any meal and it can be amplified with so many great flavours. When kale is prepared properly it can be a really relaxing process. There is a real trick to the way that kale is stripped from the stem. I've seen many chefs with whole bins full of kale stems and do not want you to make the same mistake!

You can explore different combinations of oils and salts, such as pumpkin oil and pink Himalayan salt, walnut oil and smoked salt, sesame oil and tamari, or truffle oil, salt and a pinch of cayenne pepper. Still hungry? Add a tablespoon or two of nut or seed butter once the kale is wilted and massage it through the kale for a more filling result.

PURPLE PLANTS

Roasted Red Cabbage, Black
Quinoa, Hazelnut Gremolata
and Whipped Beans

This dish celebrates the dark colours of the autumn and winter seasons. Rich in anthocyanins, which are natural pigments that make their colour, these are shown to benefit brain health and reduce inflammation. The deep roasted cabbage is contrasted with creamy garlic beans, red kale pesto and black quinoa. As always, each element can be enjoyed alone but here in this dish, you can get your anthocyanin hit and also enjoy a unique plate that's as dark as the night but good for the soul.

Serves: 4

Time taken: 45 minutes

1 medium red cabbage, outer leaves
    removed and sliced lengthways into
    4–6 rounds
100ml (scant ½ cup) olive oil or
    hazelnut oil
1 red onion, peeled and chopped
150g (scant 1 cup) black quinoa,
    rinsed and drained
1 rosemary sprig
Salt

For the hazelnut gremolata
100g (¾ cup) hazelnuts
20g (¼ cup) parsley, washed and dried
50g (1 cup) red kale, washed and dried
1 garlic clove
2 tbsp nutritional yeast
¼ tsp dried chilli flakes
Grated zest and juice of 1 lemon
5 tbsp olive oil

For the whipped beans
1 × 400g (14oz) tin of white beans,
    drained and rinsed
1 smoked garlic clove, or 1 roasted garlic clove
    with a pinch of smoked salt
100g (scant ½ cup) dark tahini
1 tbsp white miso
¾ tsp salt

"Never doubt that a small group of thoughtful committed citizens can change the world. Indeed it's the only thing that has"

—Margaret Mead

Preheat the oven to 200°C fan (220°C/425°F/Gas 7).

Place the rounds of cabbage on a large baking tray, sprinkle them with a little salt and then generously drizzle over 4–5 tablespoons of the oil, making sure each piece is coated in salt and oil. Bake for 45 minutes until lightly golden and you can easily pierce a knife through the flesh.

HAZELNUT GREMOLATA Begin making the hazelnut gremolata. Place the hazelnuts on a small baking tray and bake for 10 minutes. Leave them to cool slightly.

Next, make the quinoa. Place a medium saucepan over a low heat and add 2 tablespoons of the remaining olive oil. Once the oil is hot, add the red onion with a pinch of salt and cook for 5 minutes until translucent.

Add the quinoa to the pan and stir through the onions. Add the rosemary and 400ml (1⅔ cups) of boiling water. Cook for 10 minutes with the lid on, simmering the whole time, then check that the quinoa is done by tasting it and looking to see that the seeds have fully opened. If they have, then turn off the heat and set aside with a piece of kitchen paper under the lid. This helps the quinoa to finish cooking and steam. If the seeds haven't fully opened, give the quinoa another couple of minutes to finish cooking. Leave the quinoa like this while the rest of the elements come together.

WHIPPED BEANS To make the whipped beans, place all of the ingredients in a food processor or blender and blend until very smooth. Pour in 100ml (scant ½ cup) of cold water to help the mixture become smooth. Taste for seasoning – the beans should be creamy and salty with a good texture. Transfer to a sealed container in the fridge until you are ready to serve.

HAZELNUT GREMOLATA To finish making the hazelnut gremolata, put the roasted hazelnuts, parsley, kale and garlic in a food processor or blender and process everything until roughly broken down. Add the nutritional yeast, chilli, lemon juice and lemon zest with a good pinch of salt and process, pouring in the oil as the mixture moves. Taste for seasoning and then set it to one side.

The cabbage should by this time be cooked, the quinoa soft, the whipped beans cool and the hazelnut gremolata ready to go. To serve, take the cabbage from the oven and set it to one side. Place the beans on the base of the plate, followed by the quinoa and then the gremolata. A grinding of black pepper and a glug of olive oil will set the cabbage off just right.

Overleaf, clockwise from bottom left:
Purple Plants, Pumpkin Arancini and
Spiced Squash.

SPICED SQUASH

with Kombucha Chimichurri,
Chilli Cultured Cream and
Fried Kale Chips

This is a recipe created to celebrate the autumn season. Slow-cooked winter squash is cooked with aromatic spices and tangy fermented elements, all boosted with CBD to bring a moment of comfort and calm to any autumn day. The kale chips are an incredible addition to many dishes and also a great starter or snack.

Serves: 4
Time taken: 90 minutes

1kg (35oz) Crown Prince, butternut or onion
    squash, roughly chopped into small chunks
4 tbsp olive oil
2 tbsp maple syrup
2 tbsp coconut oil
3 star anise
1 garlic clove, lightly crushed
1 tbsp smoked paprika
¼ tsp smoked salt
Kombucha Chimichurri (see page 175) and
    Chilli Cultured Cream (see page 174),
    to serve

For the chilli nut butter
100g (scant ½ cup) almond butter
50ml (scant ¼ cup) water
½ tsp cayenne pepper
¼ tsp salt

For the fried kale chips
150g (5½oz) chickpea flour
1 tsp turmeric
Pinch of salt
Pinch of black pepper
1 litre (1 quart) sunflower oil, for frying
250g (6¼ cups) kale, washed and
    leaves stripped from the stems

TIP – Try adding cooked quinoa instead of the fried kale to this dish for a meal that can be served cool and prepared ahead of time.

Preheat the oven to 170°C fan (190°C/375°F/Gas 5). Line a baking tray with a piece of baking paper, large enough to seal around the squash so that it cooks en papillote (in a parcel). Place the squash pieces onto the lined tray.

Mix the rest of the ingredients together with 4 tablespoons of water and pour the marinade over the squash. Seal the baking paper tightly around the squash and bake for 20 minutes in the oven. Briefly take the squash from the oven and open the baking paper, then bake again for another 20 minutes until golden.

CHILLI NUT BUTTER Meanwhile, make the chilli nut butter. Place all of the ingredients into a bowl and mix well to combine. Store in the fridge until ready to use.

KALE CHIPS To make the kale chips, first place one-third of the chickpea flour in a bowl and the rest in another. Leave one bowl of flour plain and add the turmeric, salt and pepper to the other. Gradually add 100ml (scant ½ cup) of water to the seasoned flour and mix to make a smooth batter.

Place the sunflower oil in a small saucepan and slowly bring up to 170°C (325°F). Place a piece of kitchen paper on a plate next to the oil for the fried kale.

Coat each piece of kale one by one, first in the flour and then in the batter. Carefully add the coated kale pieces to the hot oil and fry them for 20 seconds on each side. Remove from the oil and place on the kitchen paper to drain. Repeat for each piece of kale. You can use this oil for frying once or twice more, as you see fit.

To serve, place the chilli nut butter on the plate, followed by the warm squash. Spoon a teaspoon of Kombucha Chimichurri onto each piece of squash, followed by the Chilli Cultured Cream and the crunchy kale. Enjoy the wow factor!

PUMPKIN ARANCINI

with Greens, Mung Bean Guacamole and Tomatoes

These pumpkin arancini were created as a way to use up leftover brown rice and went down well. Traditionally made with cheese and Arborio rice, this Mind Food version uses pumpkin, brown rice and hemp pesto to bond the rice together. The star of this plate is a mung bean guacamole, inspired by my great friend Priscilla who first made these on a cook along we did together. Why is this a Mind Food dish? It has healthy fats, whole grain brown rice loaded with rainbow vegetables, and most of all it's really enjoyable to make.

Makes: 9–11 arancini / **Serves:** 3–4
Time taken: 1 hour

100g (3½oz) squash (see Tip),
    cut into small pieces
4 tbsp olive oil
350g (12oz) cooked short grain
    brown rice (see page 182)
1 tbsp white miso
Hemp and Parsley Pesto (see page 175)
    or Chilli Cultured Cream (see page
    174), for filling (optional)
1 piece or around 100g (3½oz)
    gluten-free bread
2 tbsp nutritional yeast

For the tomatoes and greens
10 cherry tomatoes
3 tbsp olive oil
½ tsp salt
100g (1½ cups) mixed leaves, washed

For the mung bean guacamole
100g (3½oz) sprouted mung beans
    (see note on sprouting, page 23)
1 small avocado
30g (⅓ cup) parsley
1 garlic clove
Zest and juice of 1 lemon
1 tsp dried chilli flakes
½ tsp salt

Preheat the oven to 180°C fan (200°C/400°F/Gas 6).

ARANCINI First, make the arancini. Place the squash on a baking tray and drizzle over 1 tablespoon of the oil and 2 tablespoons of water. Roast for 20 minutes until soft. Leave it to cool slightly and then blend or process it into a smooth purée.

Mix the rice with the miso and squash and make balls the size of an avocado stone. The squash will help it to stick together as short grain brown rice tends to be less sticky.

If you choose to fill the arancini, add ½ teaspoon of the Hemp and Parsley Pesto or Chilli Cultured Cream into the middle of each ball. Do this by flattening the rice, adding the filling and then reshaping the arancini around it.

Place the bread in a food processor or blender with the nutritional yeast and blend into breadcrumbs. Pour the crumbs onto a small plate.

Roll each arancini in the breadcrumbs making sure they are evenly coated; the crumbs should stick quite easily to the arancini.

Drizzle the remaining oil over a baking tray and place the arancini in the tray, slightly spread out. Bake for 30 minutes until golden on each side, rotating them halfway through.

TOMATOES Meanwhile, prepare the tomatoes by cutting each one in half and tossing them with half of the olive oil and salt. Place the tomatoes on a lined baking tray and bake for 20 minutes until soft and caramelized.

Wash the leaves at this moment, but don't dress them until you are ready to serve.

GUACAMOLE Make the guacamole by adding all of the ingredients to a food processor or blender and processing until smooth. Taste to check it is nicely lemony and salty and if you need a little more seasoning, add it now. Set the guacamole to one side or place in a sealed container in the fridge if you are going to be a while.

Place a spoonful of the guacamole on each plate and slightly spread it out. Scatter a few hot tomatoes on top, then 2–3 arancini, then the leaves and finally drizzle with oil and salt.

TIP – It is useful to have roasted squash to hand to use in salads or dishes like this. If you have pre-roasted squash to hand in your fridge, use that and blend it up straight away, skipping the squash cooking process.

If you don't have sprouted mung beans you can use pumpkin seeds or hemp seeds in their place.

TWO WAYS
WITH POLENTA

Polenta is a wonderfully satisfying ingredient that is also very versatile, so prepare it ahead of time and you can have meals for a week. Polenta is a 'flour' made from corn, which is one of the world's most widely used ingredients. As with all ingredients, it is important to ensure you use the best possible quality.

In these recipes, you will see how to make 'wet' and 'set' polenta dishes and from here there are so many tremendous possibilities. The main Mind Food benefit is that you have a satiating meal, which is grounding, tasty and inexpensive to make.

SESAME POLENTA WITH AUBERGINE CAPONATA

This recipe is a Mind Food sort of comfort food. The two parts to this plate contrast perfectly, with the polenta being creamy and salty against the warm, rich, sweet tomato caponata. Oregano can be useful for digestion, hence its use in many Spanish and Greek dishes. This dish will hopefully transport you to a cool Mediterranean evening.

Serves: 2

Time taken: 45 minutes

100g (⅔ cup) polenta
750ml (generous 3 cups) vegetable
    stock or water
5 tbsp nutritional yeast
1 rosemary sprig, finely chopped
50g (1¾oz) plant-based butter
3 tbsp tahini
Salt and freshly ground black pepper

For the aubergine caponata

4 tbsp olive oil
2 aubergines (eggplants), washed and
    cut into 2cm (¾in) cubes
½ tsp salt
1 red onion, finely sliced
2 tbsp smoked paprika
2 garlic clove, crushed
400ml (14fl oz) passata
100ml (scant ½ cup) vegetable stock
    or water
2 tbsp capers
1 tbsp dried oregano

POLENTA Start by heating a large saucepan over a medium heat. Add the polenta and lightly toast it before adding the stock or water, 250ml (1 cup) at a time. Keep stirring to check there are no lumps. Continue this process for about 20 minutes.

AUBERGINE CAPONATA While the polenta is cooking, place a frying pan over a medium heat and add the oil. Once the oil is hot, add the aubergine with the salt and fry until bronzed on each side (about 10 minutes). Add the onion and cook for a couple more minutes until the onion is soft. Add the smoked paprika and garlic, then cook for a further minute.

Add the passata and stock or water, then simmer for 20 minutes, by which time you should have a thick and glossy sauce. Add the capers and oregano and cook for a final 5 minutes. The sauce should be sweet and salty with a good flavour of the onions and smoked paprika.

POLENTA Finish the polenta by adding the nutritional yeast, rosemary and butter, with a pinch of salt and pepper. Mix together and taste to check the seasoning.

Serve a good ladleful of the polenta on a plate, topped with the caponata.

TIP – Pour any leftover polenta into a non-stick baking tray and leave to set and cool to be enjoyed the next day.

POLENTA CHIPS

with Red Pepper Ketchup

This set polenta is wonderfully comforting, served like chips with cheese and sauce. Instead of cutting this set polenta like chips, you can also enjoy it cut into larger squares or triangles with the caponata, as opposite, tomato sauces, salads and so many other ingredients. Think of it variously as a base/chip/toast and let your imagination run wild.

Serves: 4

Time taken: 45 minutes

100ml (scant ½ cup) olive oil or neutral oil
1 tray of set polenta, cut into thick
    chip shapes
5 macadamia nuts, grated, to serve
Salt

For the red pepper ketchup

1 red pepper
2 tbsp olive oil
1 white onion
100g (3½oz) passata
1 tbsp Clever Kimchi (see page 161)
    or store-bought kimchi

Preheat the oven to 200°C fan (220°C/425°F/Gas 7).

KETCHUP First, start preparing the red pepper ketchup. Place the pepper whole on a baking tray and roast until it has darkened, at least 30 minutes. Remove from the oven and set aside to cool.

POLENTA CHIPS Turn the oven down to 180°C fan (200°C/400°F/Gas 6). Add the oil to a large baking tray and place it in the oven to heat. After a couple of minutes, when the oil is hot, add the polenta chips to the tray, being VERY cautious not to let the hot oil splash. Bake for 40 minutes, turning the polenta chips onto a different side every 10 minutes.

KETCHUP Finish making the red pepper ketchup. Heat the olive oil in a small saucepan with a pinch of salt. Add the onion and cook slowly until softened. After 10 minutes, add the passata and simmer for 2 minutes. Cool the mixture, then once the roasted pepper has cooled, carefully peel the skin and remove the stem and seeds (any remaining seeds will make the ketchup taste bitter).

Blend the pepper with the onion mixture and the kimchi until they are very smooth. Pour the pepper ketchup back into the frying pan and simmer for 10 minutes until reduced a little more. Remove from the heat and leave the ketchup to cool. Store the ketchup in a sealed container in the fridge until everything else is ready.

Once gorgeously golden, remove the polenta chips from the oven, then plate them covered in grated macadamia nuts, extra salt and a serving of the stunning red pepper ketchup.

THE MIND FOOD FRY-UP

Qi Beans, Scrambled Tofu,
Caramelized Tomatoes and
Smoked Mushrooms

This Mind Food Fry Up is a real morning treat, with extra bean power from the Qi beans. These are the most delicious beans I've ever made. Admittedly, more elaborate than your average bean but perfect for a quick and satisfying meal made ahead of time and served on toast, pancakes, or with fresh crusty bread. 'Qi', pronounced 'chi', meaning energy, is exactly what these beans give you, with flavour and fibre to see you through the day.

Serves: 2
Time taken: 45 minutes

For the Qi beans

2 tbsp olive oil
1 red onion, finely sliced
Pinch of salt
1 carrot, finely diced
1 celery stick, finely diced
1 garlic clove, crushed
3 tbsp tomato purée
1 tsp white miso
1½ tbsp harissa or Hot Sauce (see page 174)
200ml (7fl oz) passata
400g (14oz) white butter beans, canned
    and drained
125g (4oz) Clever Kimchi (see page 161)

For the caramelized tomatoes

2 tbsp olive oil
4 medium sized tomatoes, halved
¼ tsp salt

For the scrambled tofu

250g (8¾oz) firm tofu, drained
2 tbsp olive oil
1 tbsp nutritional yeast
1 tsp turmeric
1 tsp smoked paprika
1 pinch chilli flakes
1 tsp salt

For the smoked mushrooms

2 tbsp olive oil
250g mixed mushrooms, finely chopped
¼ tsp smoked salt
2 tbsp smoked water (optional)

QI BEANS Heat a medium saucepan with the olive oil over a medium heat. Once hot, add the onion and sauté with a good pinch of salt for 4–5 minutes until soft and translucent.

Add the carrot and celery to the saucepan and cook for 3–4 minutes until the carrot and celery are soft. Add the garlic and cook for another minute, stirring constantly to release the magnificent aroma.

Stir in the tomato purée, white miso and harissa sauce, then cook until a thick paste is produced. Add the passata with 240ml (1 cup) of water and cook until the liquid has reduced by a third. Add the beans and keep cooking for 5 more minutes to infuse. Leave to cool slightly. Once cooled a little, put a ladle of the beans in a food processor or blender and process until very smooth. Return the blended beans to the pan and stir through the beans.

CARAMELIZED TOMATOES Heat a frying pan over a high heat and add the olive oil. Sprinkle the tomatoes with salt and once the pan is hot, add the tomatoes, skin side down. Cook for 5 minutes on each side until soft and lightly caramelized.

SCRAMBLED TOFU Crumble the tofu into a small bowl and then add the rest of the scramble ingredients.

Add the tofu mix to the frying pan, being careful to keep it separate from the tomatoes.

SMOKED MUSHROOMS Pour the remaining oil to the pan and then add mushrooms and smoked salt. Cook the mushrooms and tofu until golden and add the smoked water to the mushrooms for the last minute, if using. When the mushrooms are bronzed and garlicky, and the tofu golden and lightly crisped, turn off the heat.

Remove the Qi beans from the heat and mix in the kimchi, including its brine.

Serve the beans with the tomatoes, tofu and mushrooms as they are or with some crusty toast.

TIP – If you have leftover beans they can be stored in a container once cool in the refrigerator for up to **4 days**. They are delicious with plant-based cheese on toast!

WINTER

It's surprisingly easy to find lots of hidden magic in the winter time of long dark days, a bounty of earthy vegetables and the brief opportunity to stop, even if just for a moment. Feel your own way into winter hibernation and look for moments that might give you the chance to enter into the peace that winter food can bring. Whether that is a soothing hot chocolate at the end of a long day, the chance for a very early night or a crisp winter morning walk when nobody else would dream of venturing outside.

Winter is traditionally a time for reflection in a world that rarely stops to look back. This chapter is an invitation to you to find the wisdom in reflection and explore this winter season's rituals. In the winter I treasure a much slower pace of life, Yin Yoga practices, warm foods and try to carve out a little more headspace for myself, spending time planning things to come. This time is for preparation and laying strong foundations for what's to come; try not to resist, and go within.

INGREDIENTS FOR WINTER

MAGNESIUM BATHS

Magnesium is a fantastic mineral for soothing and relaxing our muscles, and is something that a huge proportion of people are deficient in. A great way to ensure that you have a good dose of magnesium is by using it in a bath via what is known as Epsom salts, which you can find in most health food shops. You can also often find scented salts made with 100 per cent natural ingredients, but check the ingredients to ensure that they do not have anything unusual inside.

Run a warm bath with a good dose of the salts (up to 1 cup) and if your salts are plain, you could add a couple of sprigs of fresh rosemary to the bath while it is running. Lie in the bath for at least 20 minutes, playing mellow music or a soothing podcast if you wish. This ritual will make you warm and sleepy, so when you finish bathing, dry yourself thoroughly, drink plenty of water and snuggle up in bed.

YIN YOGA

This is a form of yoga where you hold poses for much longer than you do in a Flow Yoga class. The postures penetrate deep into the fascia and connective tissues of the body and can really help you to let go. If you study deeper into Yin Yoga, you might see that the places that are tight within your own body hold meanings that resonate. Tight hips correlate with headaches, stiff shoulders with stress, and so on. Here is a *Mind Food* routine for you to try, created to calm and soothe the mind, ideal at the end of the day to wind down.

Deep Breath – sitting in an easy and comfortable pose, cup your hands over your ears and exhale fully before taking a deep breath to inhale. Lightly hum – the sound vibrating in your head can help soothe the mind. Repeat this hum 3–5 times, holding it for as long as is comfortable, then repeat the exhaling and inhaling routine.

Two Twists – lie flat on your back, then shift your hips slightly to the left. Bring your left knee to your chest and roll your body to the right. At this time, the right leg can be slightly bent. Turn your head to the left and feel a long stretch along your left side. Hold this pose for 5 minutes and then go back to centre position and twist to the other side. Breathe long and deep throughout, then return to centre to reset for 1 minute before going into the next pose.

Happy Baby – lying on your back, bring both knees into your chest and then put the outsides of your hands around the outside edges of your feet. Slightly straighten your calves, so that the knees are pointing in towards your elbow and the calf at around 90 degrees. Hold this position for 5 minutes and gently rock from side to side if it is comfortable. Breathe long and deep throughout this routine, then return to the centre position to reset for a minute before going into the next pose.

Child's Pose – prepare to kneel on your knees, then keeping your hips pointing back towards your feet, lay your chest and arms forwards with your forehead on the floor. This light pressure on your forehead is very soothing and this pose also relieves tension in the hips. Stay in this position for 5 minutes, breathing slowly, then inhaling for 4 counts and exhaling for 6 counts.

When you have completed this routine, you may like to lie on your back for another minute, continuing to breathe smoothly, and just relax.

WRITING

Finding a way to write can be an incredible practice, not only to notice your own rhythms, but also to express what you're feeling or uncover thoughts you may not realize are there. There are many different ways to make this practice your own; some do 'morning pages', writing a few pages as soon as they wake up, while others keep detailed diaries of each day. I like to use a sketchpad without lines, but the main thing is simply to find what works best for you. When I'm feeling anxious or confused, writing is often when I uncover what's really going on when my words can't quite capture the reality of the day.

TOASTED WALNUT OATS AND ROSEMARY BERRIES

In the morning, when you need good support for the day, there's nothing better than porridge – a warming bowl of high fibre oats with protein-rich nuts and healthy fats. This *Mind Food* porridge is laced with our favourite *Mind Food* ingredients of Rosemary Walnuts and Rosemary Berries. These brain-boosting ingredients are here to keep you sailing through the winter season feeling good. I love to use different grains to keep it interesting and of course you can explore using different nuts and fruits as seasons change.

Serves: 2

Time taken: 15 minutes

150g (1 cup) buckwheat, quinoa, millet or oat flakes

500ml (generous 2 cups) freshly made walnut milk (see page 171) or your favourite nut milk

Large pinch of salt

1 tbsp honey

1 tbsp New-Age Nut Butter (see page 159) (optional)

1 tsp lion's mane mushroom powder (optional)

To serve

4 tbsp Antioxidant Jam (see page 154)

Handful of Rosemary Walnuts (see page 153)

Maple syrup, to taste

TOASTED OATS Make the toasted oats by heating a small saucepan over a medium heat and pouring the oats inside. Warm through for a couple of minutes until they are lightly toasted; you will know they are ready when you can smell that great flavour change. Add the nut milk and bring it to a simmer.

After 5 minutes, most of the liquid should have been absorbed. If you prefer your oats less thick, just add a little more milk or water. Season the oats and add a little honey for sweetness to match your liking.

If you want to give the oats an extra boost, take them off the heat and add New-Age Nut Butter and lion's mane powder.

Divide the mixture between two bowls and top with a couple of tablespoons of Antioxidant Jam and finish with a sprinkle of Rosemary Walnuts and a dash of maple syrup, if using. This will certainly keep you going through any dreary winter morning!

TIP – Try this recipe with sesame seed milk, tahini and fresh fruit for a springtime porridge.

SWEET POTATO AND CHILLI DAUPHINOISE

with Pumpkin Alguashte

Dauphinoise potatoes are the ultimate comfort food for this time of year, when we all need a little more light, the bright colours and spice in these potatoes help to bring a little sunshine to anyone's day. When I was studying for my degree, I would often make batches of classic dauphinoise for days when I wasn't feeling so great. Having them ready to heat when I didn't feel like cooking was such a lifesaver. This recipe is a new and improved version of the potatoes I had in those darker times.

Serves: 6
Time taken: 1 hour, plus soaking

2 tbsp olive oil
1 large red onion, finely sliced
½ tsp salt
4 garlic cloves, crushed
500g (1lb 2oz) sweet potatoes, washed and sliced into 2mm (⅛in) rounds
400g (14oz) potatoes (I like Alouettes), washed and sliced into 2mm (⅛in) rounds
200g (1⅔ cups) cashew nuts, soaked for at least 1 hour in hot water, then well rinsed
1 tsp dried chilli flakes
3 tbsp nutritional yeast
Freshly cracked black pepper

For the alguashte
100g (¾ cup) pumpkin seeds
½ tsp dried chilli flakes
½ tsp smoked salt

Preheat the oven to 180°C fan (200°C/400°F/Gas 6).

DAUPHINOISE Heat the oil in a large saucepan. Once hot, add the onion and salt. Cook over a low heat for about 10 minutes until soft, but not brown. Add the garlic and cook for a further minute.

Add all the potatoes to the pan with 400ml (generous 2 cups) of water and bring to a simmer. Simmer the potatoes for about 10 minutes.

Blend the soaked cashews with 400ml (generous 2 cups) of water in a food processor or blender for 30 seconds to make a cream.

Pour the cashew cream into the pan with the potatoes and add the chilli flakes, nutritional yeast and some black pepper. Simmer for 5 minutes until the potatoes are soft.

Tumble the cooked potatoes and creamy sauce in a medium baking tray with reasonably high sides. Make the top layer of potatoes quite neat, then place the tin in the oven to bake for 20 minutes, or until the top layer of potatoes is golden brown.

ALGUASHTE To make the alguashte, place a small saucepan over a medium heat. Add the pumpkin seeds and toast until they start to pop. Once toasted, transfer the seeds to a pestle and mortar with the chilli and salt and grind everything into a dust.

Remove the potatoes from the oven and leave them to sit for a few minutes to cool a little. You can eat the hot dauphinoise sprinkled with the alguashte just as they are, or serve with fresh leaves, grilled purple sprouting or massaged kale.

CACAO BAKED BEETROOT

This dish is both flavourful and aromatic. It is inspired by salt baked beetroot, but instead of salt, the cacao beans and spices infuse the beetroot with a rich and aromatic flavour, which is a truly unique way to enjoy this winter vegetable. With the cacao infusion going a long way to make a great flavour, you can also create a similar recipe with coffee beans. Enjoy the baked beetroot hot or cold in salads or blended into a dip.

Serves: 4
Time taken: 2 hours

500g (1lb 2oz) mixed beetroot
100g (3½oz) cacao nibs
1 tbsp fennel seeds
1 tbsp cumin seeds
1 tbsp coriander seeds
1 tsp salt
100ml (scant ½ cup) olive oil

To serve
Handful of Rosemary Walnuts (see page 153)
Watercress or salad leaves
2 tbsp Kombucha Chimichurri (see page 175)
    or Maca and Mustard Dressing
    (see page 174) (optional)
2 tbsp of sour cream (optional)

Preheat the oven to 170°C fan (190°C/375°F/Gas 5).

Do not peel the beetroot. Wash them thoroughly to remove any soil, then cut each one in half, from root to shoot, and set aside.

Line a large baking tray with a piece of baking paper large enough to cover the beetroot so that they can cook 'en papillote' (in a parcel).

Sprinkle the paper with the cacao nibs, all the seeds and the salt. Lay each beetroot on the paper, cut side down, nestling them gently into the spice mix. Drizzle with oil and 100ml (scant ½ cup) of water.

Wrap the paper around the beetroot, twisting the edges so that it closes, then twist and fold the bottom end over. Leave enough space around the food to allow the air to expand and circulate. If you have a tight seal, the package will swell up like a balloon when it cooks.

Bake for about an hour and a half. Once the beetroot is cooked through, peel off the skins when still hot, which will be easy to do.

Leave the beetroot to cool for at least 30 minutes and then finely slice each one. Lay them on a plate sprinkled with Rosemary Walnuts and watercress or salad leaves. Finish with either Kombucha Chimichurri, Maca and Mustard Dressing or sour cream (if using).

TIP – Like all the recipes in Mind Food, we are conscious of using each and every ingredient to its full. So when you have finished with the cacao nibs here, you can grind them in a pestle and mortar, then use as a rich and energizing sprinkle on salads and vegetables or bake them into savoury granolas, fold them into raw pastries or make a chocolate bark with these slightly spiced and savoury nibs scattered on top.

BRUSSELS SPROUTS A FEW WAYS

GARLIC SPROUTS

Brussels sprouts may occasionally split opinions, but they are just incredible at this time of year and there is no denying that whatever nature provides, it always has some sort of benefit for that particular time of year or season. Brussels sprouts are not just for Christmas, they are a fantastic winter green to enjoy alongside so many other plants and flavours. These recipes can be enjoyed as a side to your roast dinner or otherwise, but equally, garlic sprouts can be tossed through pasta with lemon in a whole new way.

These sprouts are so versatile. I end up eating these greens on top of Okonomiyaki (see page 103), with rice, noodles or pasta and a generous squeeze of lemon.

Serves: 4, as a side
Time taken: 20 minutes

300g (3 cups) Brussels sprouts and sprout tops if you have them, washed
50g (1¾oz) plant-based butter

50g (1¼ cups) kale, washed and stripped from the stems with the stems finely chopped
2 garlic cloves, crushed
¼ tsp salt
¼ tsp ground black pepper

Take the ends off the freshly washed sprouts, removing any discoloured outer leaves, then finely slice the sprouts into long thin pieces.

Fry in butter for a couple of moments to colour and crisp them up and add the sliced sprouts to the pan with the kale and garlic.

Cook over a medium-high heat so that everything sizzles in a wonderful way, then sprinkle with salt and pepper, shaking the pan to coat.

Once the sprouts are golden and everything is cooked through, serve hot and crispy.

ROAR SPROUTS

This is my absolute favourite way to cook sprouts with a bit of festive cheer, celebrating the humble Brussels sprout, just back in season over these winter months. They're ideal with a crisp hint of sage and to top them off, candied sweet winter chestnuts with that ROAR of lion's mane mushroom powder to bring a big apoptogenic shine to the season. Lion's mane is an amazing mushroom used to support the gut and the brain. It supports mental health while also adding a deep mushroom flavour to so many recipes.

Serves: 4, as a side
Time taken: 20 minutes

300g (3 cups) Brussels sprouts, washed
1 tbsp plant-based butter
Salt and freshly ground black pepper

For the crispy sage
3 tbsp olive oil
A good pinch of salt, preferably smoked
½ tsp maple syrup
About 40 sage leaves (5g/¼ cup)

For the lion's mane chestnuts
1 tbsp olive oil
1 tsp maple syrup
65g (⅔ cup) chestnuts, cooked
1 tbsp lion's mane mushroom powder

TIP – Have you heard of kalettes? These are perhaps my favourite vegetable – a cross between sprouts and kale that you find more and more easily now in shops and farmers' markets. Try using them in either of these Brussels sprout recipes or bake them with oil and salt for a crispy treat.

CRISPY SAGE Measure the oil, salt and maple syrup into a mixing bowl. Pick the sage leaves from the stems and place in the bowl, mixing so that the sage is well coated.

Heat a large saucepan over a high heat. Once hot, add the sage leaves, ensuring that each leaf has a bit of space in the saucepan. The sage will begin to sizzle. After about 10 seconds, turn each piece over. Once each piece of sage is lightly golden, turn them out onto a side plate. Once cool, they should be super crispy.

BRUSSELS SPROUTS Take the bottom off each sprout and if they are large, cut each one lengthways down the middle, then lengthways again to make four quarters. If smaller, just cut them in half. Remove any bruised outer leaves, but if there are any other leaves that fall off during prep, keep them to cook as they will be the tasty crispy bits!

Prepare a large bowl of cold water and set aside – this will be needed for blanching the sprouts in a moment. Set up a steamer and bring some water to the boil. Steam the sprouts for 2 minutes over a medium simmer. Toss the sprouts into the cool water, so that they won't over cook when we move onto the next step.

CHESTNUTS Place the olive oil and maple syrup into a small bowl. Add the chestnuts and squash them all slightly. Heat a frying pan over a medium heat. Once the pan is hot, add the chestnuts, then sizzle for about 5 minutes, shaking every so often. The chestnuts will then be golden and crispy. Add the lion's mane mushroom powder to the same bowl you used for the marinade, then add the candied chestnuts and toss everything together. Set these to one side and put the pan back onto the heat.

The final step is to add the sprouts to the sizzling pan with the plant-based butter. Cook over a high heat for about 3–4 minutes until the Brussels sprouts turn a beautiful bronze colour. Season with a little salt and a generous amount of black pepper. Tumble onto a bowl or plate, scatter with the candied chestnuts and top with the crispy sage. The perfect festive side!

PARSNIP FRIES WITH MISO MAYO

I love to use parsnips in many ways – as a rice, roasted in a salad or half and half with potato to make a tasty mash. The spices used on the parsnips in this recipe can help with inflammation, and the mayo benefits from light fermentation and has a sweet and salty flavour. We know by now the benefits of good bacteria for the gut. So dig into these crunchy, creamy fries and know you are doing yourself a little good in each bite.

Serves: 4, as a snack or side
Time taken: 45 minutes

2 parsnips
2 tbsp miso
¼ tsp cayenne pepper
¼ tsp ground cloves
¼ tsp turmeric
6 tbsp olive oil
Handful of parsley, to garnish
1 batch of Miso Mayo (see page 175), to serve

Preheat the oven to 170°C fan (190°C/375°F/Gas 5). Line a baking tray with baking paper.

Wash and peel the parsnips, then top and tail them before cutting each one in half and then into four long 1cm (½in) thick 'fries'.

Mix the miso and spices with 4 tablespoons of water in a bowl until smooth. Add the oil and mix again.

Drizzle half of this mixture over the parsnips making sure you thoroughly cover each of the fries.

Place the parsnips on the lined baking tray lined and bake for 20–30 minutes until golden. Every 10 minutes, paint a little more of the marinade on the parsnips and turn them onto a different side if necessary.

Once the parsnips are a gorgeously golden colour, take them from the oven and garnish with a handful of parsley. Serve hot with a spoon of the Miso Mayo!

Previous page, clockwise from top left:
Parsnip Fries with Miso Mayo, Okonomiyaki on My Mind, Roar Sprouts, Garlic Sprouts.

OKONOMIYAKI ON MY MIND

When I discovered okonomiyaki, I became slightly obsessed with it, recreating it time and time again with different vegetables and sauces. Traditionally a Japanese street food with the name derived from the word *okonomi*, meaning 'how you like' or 'what you like', and *yaki* meaning 'cooked'. I love that this dish can be what you like, as that is exactly what Mind Food is all about. I've decided to use quite traditional savoy cabbage here, but you can use vegetables like kale, ribboned carrots or anything that tickles your fancy.

Serves: 4
Time taken: 30 minutes

200g (7oz) chickpea flour
50g (1¾oz) grated vegetables, such as
    parsnips or carrots
100g Clever Kimchi (see page 161)
1 nori sheet
1 tbsp sesame oil

For the umami drizzle

150g (5½oz) New Age Nut Butter
    (see page 159)
1 tbsp white miso
1 tsp tamari
1 tsp honey
2.5cm (1in) fresh ginger, grated
¼ tsp chilli powder
1 tsp lion's mane mushroom powder
    (optional)

To serve

Spring onions, finely chopped
Handful of coriander, leaves only
1 tbsp sesame seeds, toasted

OKONOMIYAKI Whisk the chickpea flour with 200ml (scant 1 cup) of water until it is really smooth, then fold the grated vegetables and kimchi through the batter.

Fold the nori sheet in half and then in half again, then snip it into very thin pieces with scissors. Add the nori to the batter and make sure everything is well mixed.

UMAMI DRIZZLE Make the umami drizzle by whisking all of the ingredients together. Pour half of the mixture into a separate bowl and whisk it with 50ml (scant ¼ cup) of water to make one batch creamier, to contrast the two sauces.

Heat a frying pan over a medium heat and add a little of the sesame oil. Ladle a large spoonful of the batter into the frying pan, spreading it into a 1cm (½in) thick round, the size of a small plate. Cook the batter for 2 minutes on each side, or until golden.

To serve, place the cooked okonomiyaki on the plate, drizzle it with the sauces and garnish with spring onions, coriander and sesame seeds. Enjoy hot!

TIP – Alternatively, you can use Cultured Pancake Batter here (see page 169) if you have it to hand. But if you are cooking on the fly, then the batter can be quickly whipped up without fermenting.

SWEET BASIL SQUASH

This sweet basil squash is a celebration of the season, slowly roasted to intensify its sweet flavour in a salty and spicy basil marinade, and served with my favourite sprouted wild rice, in a peppery seasonal salad. The squash can be served as I have here or in smaller pieces tossed with leaves as a salad. Prepare a whole squash like this and you'll have meals for a week! If you're squashed out after a few meals you can also blend the squash into a dip with a little extra tahini and lime.

Serves: 2
Time taken: 1 hour

For the squash

200ml (scant 1 cup) tamari
200ml (scant 1 cup) sesame oil
4 tbsp honey or maple syrup
Zest and juice of 1 lime
10g (½oz) fresh ginger, grated
2 garlic cloves, crushed
Small bunch of basil, leaves picked
2 wedges of Crown Prince or onion squash
   (approx. 300g each), seeds removed

For the wild rice salad

100g (3½oz) wild rice, sprouted
   (see page 31)
100g (3½oz) red cabbage, very finely sliced
50g (1¾oz) mustard leaves or any dark
   peppery leaf

Preheat the oven to 170°C fan (190°C/375°F/Gas 5). Line a baking tray and baking paper.

SQUASH Make the marinade by placing all of the ingredients, except the basil and squash, in a glass jar and shaking thoroughly to combine. Add the basil leaves.

Place the squash onto the lined baking tray, spaced slightly apart so they have room to cook and crisp up and not just steam. Pour over three-quarters of the marinade and make sure the squash is well coated.

Bake for 35–40 minutes until soft, flipping the squash over halfway through.

WILD RICE SALAD To make the wild rice salad, toss the wild rice with the cabbage, leaves and the remaining marinade.

Place the roasted squash on plates and serve with the salad.

TIP – If you don't have sprouted wild rice, you can use cooked quinoa or toasted buckwheat.

SMOKED MUSHROOM AND CELERIAC TACOS

We are celebrating the celeriac here, which is a wonderful winter root, full of fibre and good for the gut. If you are new to celeriac, you can also use it in place of potatoes for mash, raw and thinly sliced in salads or baked as fries. There are a few parts to this dish, each one complementing the other: soft celeriac taco shells, crunchy salsa, garlicky mushrooms, greens and a good dash of sauce. Just like looking after your brain, a little care and attention does go a long way in making a good result.

Serves: 4

Time taken: 1 hour

1 celeriac, peeled and sliced into 2.5mm (⅛in)
    rounds (offcuts reserved for the salsa)
2 tbsp olive oil
Pinch of salt

For the cacao beans

2 tbsp olive oil
1 white onion, chopped
½ tsp salt
1 clove of garlic
1 × 400g (14oz) tin black beans
30g dark chocolate

For the celeriac salsa

Celeriac offcuts
1 tbsp chopped parsley
1 tsp dried chilli flakes
¼ tsp salt
1 tbsp olive oil
Zest and juice of 1 lemon

For the garlic mushrooms

1 tbsp olive oil
Selection of mushrooms, chopped into
    bite-size pieces
2 tbsp plant-based butter
1 garlic clove, crushed
1 rosemary sprig, leaves stripped and
    finely chopped

To serve

40g (1 cup) Massaged Kale (see page 178)
    with 2 tbsp walnut butter (optional)
2 tbsp sprouts or micro herbs for garnish
2 tbsp Lacto-chillies (see page 168)
2 tbsp of New Age Nut Butter (see page 159)
Handful of Rosemary Walnuts (see page 153)

Preheat the oven to 180°C fan (200°C/400°F/Gas 6). Line a baking tray with baking paper.

TACO SHELLS Place the celeriac onto the lined baking tray and drizzle with oil, salt and 2 tablespoons of water. Bake for about 20 minutes until soft. Make sure they don't overcook, since each 'taco' should be soft and slightly golden but not hard.

CACAO BEANS Heat the oil in a small saucepan and, when hot, add the chopped onion and salt and cook on a low heat for 10 minutes, until soft and translucent. Add the garlic (peeled and crushed) and cook for one more minute then add the beans and chocolate, cooking through until the chocolate is melted and the beans are hot.

CELERIAC SALSA Make the celeriac salsa by chipping the celeriac offcuts into small squares, the neater the better, which will assist you in developing good knife skills! Mix the celeriac with the rest of the salsa ingredients, then leave to sit and marinate.

GARLIC MUSHROOMS Heat a large frying pan with a splash of oil and, when hot, add the mushrooms and cook for about 5 minutes until golden. Add the butter, garlic and rosemary and cook for a further minute until the superb aroma of the garlic is released. I can smell it now!

Load each celeriac taco with cacao beans, mushrooms and salsa and add kale and any or all of the sauces suggested. Sit down, tune in and feed your mind.

DRINKS

A key cornerstone of Mind Food is hydration. Our brains are made up of around 75 per cent water so being hydrated is crucial. Water quality is always important to bear in mind, but did you know that water isn't always the best choice when looking for overall hydration through the day? In fact, drinking a balance of herbal teas, infused waters and fermented drinks is a good way to bring the most benefit to your brain.

Do remember, however, to avoid sugary or processed drinks. Like any overly processed ingredient, these will not do you good, and I guarantee that you can get much better sensations from the following recipes. There are drinks to suit every mood, whether you are looking to unwind or to be refreshed, so take a look through and find the one that suits you.

Some of the drinks here are also a great way to optimize your energy and nutrition. The smoothies and lattes provide a great opportunity to add an adaptogen or another portion of fruit or veg to your diet, which is always a good idea! These plants are your apothecary and these recipes are here to bring out your inner wizard, so go ahead and create.

ANYTIME TEA

This tea lifts any moment, giving a little burst of energy and providing a little sunshine in dark winter months. I love to make a big brew of this and enjoy it hot or cold, day or night, sunshine or showers. Goji berries are full of antioxidants, and said to be great for building good circulation.

Makes: 1 litre (1¾ pints)
Time taken: 10 minutes

3 tbsp goji berries
2.5cm (1in) piece of fresh ginger, cut into thin rounds
2.5cm (1in) piece of fresh turmeric
1 lemon, sliced into thin rounds
4 cups (1 litre) boiling water

Add all of the ingredients to a large heatproof teapot or jug and then pour over the boiling water. Leave to brew for at least 5 minutes before sipping.

You can enjoy this tea throughout the day, hot or cold, and top up the same infusion at least five times, nibbling on the goji berries as you sip.

Variation – if you would like to add a little bit of sparkle to your day, brew these ingredients with just half the water and leave them to cool, then top up with plain kombucha or sparkling water for a very uplifting tonic.

MUSHROOM POTION

Medicinal mushrooms are no more potent than in this tonic. If you need a boost of creativity, this drink is for you with lion's mane powder for deep focus, chaga powder for stability and coffee for that extra buzz. If you are looking for a more mellow experience, remove the coffee and swap the chaga mushroom powder for a teaspoon of reishi mushroom powder and a teaspoon of honey, which is more relaxing.

Makes: 1 cup
Time taken: 5 minutes

1 tsp chaga mushroom powder
1 tsp lion's mane powder
200ml (scant 1 cup) almond or oat milk
100ml (scant ½ cup) brewed black coffee
1 tsp honey (optional)

Add both powders to a small saucepan with the milk and whisk them to combine, making sure there are no lumps. Add the coffee and bring to a simmer.

Once the milk is simmering and everything is well combined, pour this latte into your favourite mug and enjoy.

TIP – I love to make these milky drinks in a milk frother for that real latte experience, or you can blend all of the ingredients in a food processor or blender and enjoy them over ice on a hot day.

SUNSHINE CUP

CHILLED CHOCOLATE

Saffron is an ingredient that is currently getting a lot of attention because of research showing that it provides benefits for the brain. This ancient spice has been said to increase dopamine and as the sunshine spice, what else would you expect?

I have used a good dose of saffron in this drink for a more medicinal experience, but you could use a tiny pinch and still get a nice flavour and feel.

Makes: 1 cup
Time taken: 5 minutes

150ml (⅔ cup) boiling water
3–4 saffron threads
2.5cm (1in) piece of fresh ginger, cut into smaller pieces
    (or ¼ tsp ground ginger)
2 cardamom pods, lightly crushed
150ml (⅔ cup) almond or oat milk
½ tsp honey

Add all of the ingredients to a small saucepan and simmer for 10 minutes until the liquid is wonderfully scented and golden. Strain the spices from the liquid, pour into a cup and take a little time to unwind.

Overleaf, clockwise from top right: Chilled Chocolate, Mushroom Potion, A Mug of Gold, Anytime Tea, Matcha for the Mind and Sunshine Cup.

Make and drink this hot chocolate to bring a moment of calm to your day. The combination of calming rose water and CBD oil is here to balance blissful cacao and both taste equally comforting. However, since cacao itself is a stimulant, this is one to avoid near bedtime if you have trouble sleeping.

Makes: 1 cup
Time taken: 5 minutes

30g (¼ cup) almonds, soaked for at least 2 hours in hot water
100ml (scant ½ cup) filtered water
1 tbsp cacao powder
1 tbsp carob powder
1 tbsp maple syrup
1 pipette CBD
1 cardamom pod
½ tsp rose water
Pinch of sea salt

Rinse the almonds very well and then transfer them to a high powered food processor or blender with all the remaining ingredients and blend until smooth. If your blender is not high powered, you will need to pass the mixture through a nut milk bag or fine sieve.

Once the mixture is blended, either warm through in a saucepan over a low heat, or keep cool and serve over ice.

Serve up and take a little time to chill.

A MUG OF GOLD

HEMP HOT TODDY

This is a Mind Food take on a golden milk, with extra spices known for their anti-inflammatory benefits, and which we know also have a positive effect on our gut and our brain.

When the days get cooler, this piping hot apple juice is a wonderful go-to. Laced with CBD and a zing of lemon, this is an apple juice upgrade if there ever was one.

Makes: 1 cup
Time taken: 5 minutes

1 tsp fennel seeds
3 cardamom pods, crushed
250ml (generous 1 cup) almond or oat milk
1 tsp turmeric
2.5cm (1in) piece of fresh ginger, chopped into thin strips
½ tsp honey
Pinch of black pepper
Pinch of salt

Serves: 2
Time taken: 5 minutes

1 lemon
1 cinnamon stick
500ml (2 cups) apple juice
2 pipettes CBD

Toast the fennel seeds and cardamom pods in a frying pan to release their amazing aromas.

Add all of the ingredients to a small saucepan and simmer for 15 minutes. Make sure the spices have nicely infused in the milk.

Strain the spices from the milk by passing them through a sieve and then serve in a cup and take a little time to unwind.

TIP – Make a large batch of this chai drink and enjoy it hot or cold or even spiked with a shot of coffee for a dirty chai.

First, take one thin peel of the lemon rind. Then, toast the cinnamon stick and lemon rind in a dry frying pan over a low heat to release the amazing aroma.

Pour the apple juice and CBD into a saucepan and heat over a gentle heat and whisk until warmed through.

Choose your favourite cups; something heatproof but transparent works well. Halve the lemon piece and break the cinnamon stick in two, then add them to each cup and pour over the warmed CBD and apple juice. Finish with a squeeze of lemon juice to serve.

MELLOW MOJITO

MATCHA FOR THE MIND

I drink a little alcohol on occasions but I am as happy without. Enjoying a glass of wine with friends or a few cocktails in the moonlight can be great, but drinking too much alcohol is definitely something that can mask or accentuate pains and problems for so many people. I hope that this recipe, and many others in this book, respectfully provide you with good non-alcoholic alternatives.

Matcha is a high-grade whole leaf green tea which comes as a bright green powder. It contains theanine which is a natural amino acid said to boost a feeling of calm. Although caffeinated, this recipe uses CBD to balance this out, and mint to bring an additional sense of calm. I've included tocotrienols as an optional ingredient as they make lattes exceptionally creamy and are extremely rich in vitamin E.

Serves: 2
Time taken: 5 minutes

100g (1¼ cups) frozen raspberries
2 tsp coconut sugar
Handful of ice cubes
Juice of half a lime
1 tbsp apple cider vinegar
1 mint sprig, leaves picked
250ml (1 cup) Rosemary
and Raspberry Kombucha (see page 163)
150ml (⅔cup) sparkling water

To serve
Twist of lime zest
A couple of fresh raspberries (optional)

Makes: 1 cup
Time taken: 5 minutes

1 tsp matcha
1 tbsp tocotrienols (optional)
1 pipette CBD
1 drop peppermint essence (extract)
250ml coconut milk

First muddle the raspberries with the sugar, ice, lime juice, apple cider vinegar and all but two leaves of mint. Crush everything, making sure to pop the berries.

Pour in the kombucha and sparkling water and mix everything together well. Pour into cold glasses and garnish with the remaining mint leaves, a twist of lime zest and the fresh raspberries (if using). Take time to relax and enjoy.

TIP – This is the perfect opportunity for a dash of CBD, so try adding some to your drink for an extra mellow tipple.

Add the matcha and tocotrienols to a small bowl that you can drink from and preferably hold in both hands. Add a splash of milk or water and whisk with a matcha or balloon whisk for a smooth texture, making sure the mixture is frothy and smooth.

Top the drink up with cold or hot water depending on what you need and then add the CBD, peppermint and milk (again, this can be cold or warm). Make sure everything is mixed, then sit down, take a deep breath and slowly sip.

PUCKER-UP MIMOSA

This is a sharp and sweet drink that is exceptionally refreshing. I love this drink especially served very cold on a hot day. Citrus is full of vitamin C and many minerals that support our brain health. But its overall effect in this recipe is to leave us feeling totally refreshed.

Serves: 2
Time taken: 5 minutes

1 lemon
1 orange
2.5cm (1in) piece of fresh turmeric or 60ml (¼ cup) of Ginger Bug
    (see page 164) (optional but amazing)
150ml (⅔ cup) Plain Kombucha (see page 162)
100ml (generous ⅓ cup) sparkling water
1–2 tsp honey or agave
Pinch of salt
Dried chilli flakes, to taste
Ice cubes (optional)

Squeeze the juice of the lemon, orange and turmeric through a juicer over a large bowl or jug. Alternatively, blend them together in a food processor or blender and then pass through a nut milk bag or fine muslin cloth.

Pour in the kombucha and sparkling water and add the honey, salt and chilli. Top up with ice if you would like this drink extra cool. Serve in two cold glasses and pucker up.

TIP – You could put sugar and salt around the rim of the glasses if you're feeling fancy.

MAGIC MILK

Whether you're heading to a summer festival or an evening picnic, this plant-based, mood-boosting drink will keep you energized. This milk is designed to keep you dancing through the night; think of it as your new espresso martini.

It's a fantastic natural lift with mood boosters and it never fails to keep me skipping through the fields.

Makes: 1 cup
Time taken: 5 minutes

1 tbsp cacao powder
1 tsp maca powder
1 tsp honey
Pinch of salt
120ml (½ cup) cold brew coffee
    (or brewed regular coffee if cold brew isn't available)
240ml (1 cup) plant-based milk
Ice cubes (optional)

Put the cacao and maca in a cup with the honey and salt and 1 tablespoon of the coffee. Stir it well to form a paste and remove any lumps from the powders.

Add the rest of the coffee, the milk and the cacao paste to a cocktail shaker and shake well over ice, if using. If you are out and about, away from utensils, pour everything into a jar or bottle and shake well.

Sip, savour and go wild.

Opposite from top left: Mellow Mojito, Magic Milk, Hemp Hot Toddy and Pucker-Up Mimosa.

SMOOTHIES

Smoothies are a great and quick way to start the morning and I hope these Mind Food blends take your smoothie experience to the next level. Being organized can stave off hunger on any busy morning so although these are ideally made fresh, they are also good made the night before. Each one has different benefits to suit your mood or the season, so go with how you're feeling and always think ahead!

Serves: 1–2
Time taken: 5 minutes each

METHOD With each recipe, simply blend the ingredients together for at least 30 seconds until you know everything is smooth. Serve with a sprinkle of bee pollen, hemp seeds, cacao nibs or just as they are. Each recipe will serve 1 hungry person or even 2 who might decide to have something else as well for breakfast.

BERRY-BEET (CHILL)

250ml (1 cup) water
100g (1 cup) blackcurrants
3 tbsp hemp seeds
50g (1¾oz) beetroot, washed,
　　peeled and chopped into small pieces
1 pipette CBD
¼ tsp vanilla powder
⅛ tsp salt
Honey, to taste (optional)

GRASSHOPPER (BALANCE)

250ml (1 cup) cooled green tea or water
30g (1oz) frozen peas
Handful of greens, such as kale or
　　spinach, thoroughly washed
1 apple or pear, washed and cored
30g (1oz) pistachio butter or nuts
30g (1oz) fennel
Juice of half a lemon
2–3 parsley stems

DIGESTIVE (SOOTHE)

250ml (1 cup) water
4 tbsp tahini
100g (1¼ cups) frozen raspberries
2 dried figs
1 tbsp fennel seeds
1 tsp ashwagandha (optional)
⅛ tsp salt

JUNGLE JUICE (LIFT)

250ml (1 cup) water
100g (3½oz) squash, butternut or
　　Crown Prince, chopped
50g (1¾oz) goji berries
1 banana, frozen
2 tbsp coconut yoghurt
3 Brazil nuts
1 tsp turmeric
1 tsp lucuma or maca powder (optional)
Pinch of cayenne pepper
⅛ tsp salt

SECRET REMEDY (BALANCE)

250ml (1 cup) cooled green tea or water
100g (3½oz) frozen blueberries and
　　or blackberries
1 frozen banana
3 tbsp almond butter
1 tbsp carob powder
1 tsp charcoal powder
1 tsp acai powder (optional)
⅛ tsp salt

THINKING TONIC (FOCUS)

100ml (scant ½ cup) cooled brewed
　　coffee or cold brew coffee
1 banana, frozen
2 tbsp New Age Nut Butter
　　(see page 159)
150ml (⅔ cup) walnut milk (see page 171),
　　or 2 tbsp walnut butter with 150 ml
　　(⅔ cup) water
3 dates, pitted and soaked
2 tbsp cacao powder
1 tsp carob powder (optional)
1 tsp lion's mane mushroom powder
⅛ tsp salt

Mind Food is about giving yourself what you need and it can certainly include sweet treats that create a moment of calm or comfort. You will see that all of these desserts use whole ingredients, dried fruits, nuts and seeds to create decadent and delicious results. We can be so habitual in what we have to eat or think we need, but often shaking things up provides the change we may have been searching for. Occasionally, I think if something just isn't working or indeed doesn't feel right, do the opposite and see what happens.

Remember, as with anything, moderation is key. Find a moment in your day mid-morning or afternoon for these treats and take even just a few seconds to really savour them. After all, *how* we eat is just as important as *what* we eat.

The whole idea is to rediscover your favourite things, reimagine what your own 'normal' really is and understand what is possible in food and in life.

MELTDOWN MOMENTS

To me, there is nothing more satisfying than a soft chocolate. Cacao has many benefits, is packed full of a unique blend of minerals including magnesium, and also contains anandamide, which is known as the bliss chemical. The name comes from the Sanskrit word *ananda*, meaning 'joy, bliss and delight' and is also produced naturally in the brain. These melting pralines are one of my favourite sweet treats. For that instant boost they can be made to suit any mood. Explore these different combinations and find the one that works best for you.

Makes: 10

Time taken: 10 minutes,
    plus 4–5 hours setting time

SOOTHE

70g (⅓ cup) Brazil nut butter
50g (¼ cup) maple syrup
40g (4 tbsp) melted chocolate
⅛ tsp sea salt
10 tart cherries, pitted
    (to press into each praline before it sets)
100g (3½oz) plant-based chocolate, for enrobing

CHILL

70g (⅓ cup) Hemp Butter
    (see page 158)
50g (¼ cup) maple syrup
40g (4 tbsp) melted chocolate
1 tsp CBD
¼ tsp sea salt
100g (3½oz) plant-based chocolate, for enrobing

LIFT

70g (⅓ cup) almond butter
50g (¼ cup) honey
40g (4 tbsp) melted chocolate
1 tsp maca powder
¼ tsp sea salt
½ tsp cayenne pepper
100g (3½oz) plant-based chocolate, for enrobing

BALANCE

70g (⅓ cup) pumpkin seed butter
50g (¼ cup) maple syrup
40g (4 tbsp) melted chocolate
½ tsp tamari
100g (3½oz) plant-based chocolate, for enrobing

FOCUS

70g (⅓ cup) walnut butter
50g (¼ cup) maple syrup
40g (4 tbsp) melted chocolate
1 tsp lion's mane mushroom powder
¼ tsp sea salt
100g (3½oz) plant-based chocolate, for enrobing

"If you don't go within you go without"

—Magdalena Gladstone

Make sure that all of the ingredients are at room temperature before starting this recipe. If anything is cold and comes into contact with the chocolate, you will notice that it seizes up and will not be possible to blend.

Whisk together all ingredients or process them in a small food processor or blender, making sure that everything is well combined. Pour the mixture into a silicone or chocolate mould. You could also pour the mixture into a small container to set and then roll it into balls or cut it into cubes, once set.

Once the pralines are set, enrobe them in chocolate.

To enrobe your pralines, finely slice the enrobing chocolate and place it in a small heatproof bowl. Bringing a saucepan half full of water up to the boil, place the heatproof bowl on top and turn down the heat. Keep an eye on the chocolate and gently stir to melt it. Once melted, take the bowl from the heat, ready for the next step, making sure the chocolate isn't too hot.

Take each praline out of the mould and then, one by one, submerge them in the melted chocolate. Make sure that they are all evenly coated and then, with a fork or chocolate wand, take them out of the melted chocolate, making sure that the fork is touching

their bases rather than the top or you will get a fork imprint in the end result. Tap off any excess chocolate on the side of the bowl and place each one on a piece of baking paper to fully set.

When the chocolate has set around the melting moment praline, sprinkle them with cacao powder or edible glitter, or leave plain and store in the fridge. They will keep in a sealed container for up to 2 weeks.

CRANBERRY AND TAHINI TRUFFLES

Truffles have been such a staple at my events and dinners over the years. I often think there's nothing better after dinner than just one – or maybe two – soft and luxurious truffles. They are so easy to make and can be made in hundreds of different flavours. Our Mind Food truffle is this more-ish tahini and cranberry flavour. Tahini is such a great base with a distinct flavour that blends well with the cacao and enrobes the tart cranberries to produce a very simple but great surprise.

Makes: 10–15 truffles

Time taken: 20 minutes, plus 4 hours refrigeration

225g (8oz) tahini

50g (¼ cup) maple syrup

¼ tsp vanilla extract

50ml (scant ¼ cup) plant-based milk (almond or oat work well)

1 tsp tamari

½ tsp cayenne pepper

2 tbsp cacao powder

1 tablespoon carob powder, plus extra to coat

100g (½ cup plus 1 tablespoon) cacao butter, melted

30 dried cranberries

Add the tahini, maple syrup, vanilla extract, milk, tamari and cayenne pepper to a bowl or blender and mix thoroughly. Add the cacao and carob powders and mix or blend once more. Slowly pour in the melted cacao butter and blend until well combined.

Place the mixture in a container and refrigerate for 2 hours to firm. Scoop the mixture into individual balls and place 2 cranberries inside each one. Roll them in carob powder to coat.

Place the truffles on a plate or baking tray and leave in the fridge for 2 hours. Once set, store in a sealed container in the fridge for up to 1 week or in the freezer for up to 1 month (if they last that long!)

TIP – Try these truffles with any nut butter and make a variety of different flavours!

OMEGA SEED AND GOJI BERRY ROCKY ROAD

This rocky road makes the perfect staple snack. With natural ingredients that really hit the sweet spot, it provides a great kick for any time of day. Packed full of seeds and nutrient-dense fruit with an extra boost from the medicinal mushrooms, this is a Mind Food snack if there ever was one! The best bit is that this dessert is quick to make and will be set in the fridge after just a couple of hours.

Makes: 10 squares
Time taken: 4 hours

100g (scant ½ cup) nut butter
2–3 tbsp molasses (any liquid sweetener
    will work but molasses adds a
    wonderful richness)
¼ tsp salt
20g (¾oz) dark carob powder
    (use cacao if you can't find carob)
1 tbsp reishi or chaga mushroom powder
    (optional)
30g (1oz) coconut oil, melted
30g (1oz) dried fruit (goji berries or mulberries
    are really nice)
40g (1½oz) seeds (hemp and chia work well)

Mix the nut butter with the molasses, salt and 70ml (generous ¼ cup) of water in a medium bowl until you have a smooth paste.

Once the mixture is smooth and everything is well combined, add the carob powder and the reishi or chaga powder, if using, and mix again.

Gradually add the melted coconut oil and continue to stir until well combined. Once silky smooth, check the saltiness to taste, then stir through the dried fruits and seeds.

Spoon the mixture into a square tin lined with baking paper and smooth the mixture down, so that it is flat. The mixture will be quite thick, so leave it to set in the fridge for a couple of hours until firm. These will keep in the fridge in an airtight container for 1 week.

Overleaf from top left: Lunar Cookies, Meltdown Moments and Cranberry and Tahini Truffles.

TIP – Carob is a caffeine-free member of the pea family that grows around Europe and was traditionally fed as a treat to horses. Many people who grew up going to health-food shops may think of carob as something their parents would give them that was less exciting than a chocolate bar. Over the last few years, carob has hugely grown on me. It is a perfect partner to cacao, whether in drinks or desserts, but also delicious alone. I will often switch cacao for carob if I need a break from the cacao high, as carob has a wonderfully natural sweet flavour.

LUNAR COOKIES

These cookies are inspired by the concept of seed syncing, which involves eating certain seeds at particular times in your menstrual cycle. This method is reputed to help hormone imbalances, regulate monthly cycles, minimize mood swings and reduce hormone-related pain. Hormone health and mental health are of course entwined – if one is out of balance it has an impact on the other, so knowing our triggers can be hugely helpful.

Makes: 7 cookies
Time taken: 30 minutes

40g (1½oz) ground pumpkin seeds
   (follicular) or sesame seeds (luteal)
2 tbsp flax seeds (follicular) or
   esame (luteal)
40g (scant ½ cup) gluten-free oats or
   millet flakes
40g (1½oz) coconut oil or plant-based butter
1 tsp white miso
2 tsp maple syrup
1 tbsp rapadura sugar
¼ tsp vanilla (follicular) or
   1 tsp ginger powder (luteal)
¼ tsp moringa (follicular) or matcha (luteal)
1 tbsp water
½ tsp baking powder
½ tsp bicarbonate of soda (baking soda)
20g white chocolate, chopped (follicular)
   dark chocolate, chopped (luteal)

Preheat the oven to 170°C fan (190°C/375°F/Gas 5). Line a baking tray with baking paper.

Place the seeds and oats together in a food processor or blender and blend them into a flour.

Place the coconut oil or plant-based butter, miso and maple syrup together in one bowl, thoroughly creaming the sugar and oil, then add the seed and oat mix along with the other remaining ingredients. Mix thoroughly to combine.

Roll the mixture into 7 evenly sized balls and place them on the lined baking tray lined with enough room for them to spread out. Lightly squash each ball.

Bake for 12 minutes until lightly golden. Once cooked, remove the cookies from the oven and leave to cool on a baking tray for at least 10 minutes, so that they firm up.

Once cool, make a cup of tea, put your feet up and dig in.

TIP – Seed syncing is a method of supporting your menstrual cycle by eating certain combinations of seeds at certain times in your cycle. The first day of your period is the follicular phase, and at this time it is helpul to eat 2 tablespoons of pumpkin seeds and 2 tablespoons of flax seeds every day. This can be in the form of a nut butter, sprinkled on salads or in recipes such as this one. In the middle of your cycle, after ovulation, is the lutial phase, when you can include 2 tablespoons of sunflower seeds and 2 tablespoons of sesame seeds. This practice can ease period pain, improve sleep and regulate cycles. You can use an app to track your cycle to better understand which phase you are in.

THAT CBD CARAMEL SHORTBREAD

This shortbread was one of the first Mind Food creations that came to exist. The super-powered recipe uses hemp in all three layers and the barley grass in the base helps with that biscuity taste. The hemp butter creates a wonderful creaminess in the caramel topped with the smooth milk chocolate CBD ganache. This shortbread has won many hearts over the years and I hope it captures yours, too.

Makes: 12
Time taken: 4 hours

For the shortbread base

150g (1½ cups) gluten-free oats
40g (scant ½ cup) coconut sugar
30g (1oz) green powder, such as barley grass
45g (1½oz) hemp seeds
Large pinch of salt
40g (1½oz) coconut oil, melted

For the hemp caramel

175g (6oz) pitted dates, soaked
100g (3½oz) Hemp Butter (see page 158)
1g vanilla extract
55g (2oz) coconut oil, melted
Pinch of salt

For the ganache

180g (6½oz) bar of vegan 75% chocolate,
   grated or finely chopped
2 tbsp hemp or olive oil
1 tbsp Hemp Butter (see page 158)
200ml (scant 1 cup) boiling water
3–5 pipettes CBD, depending on
   your CBD strength
Pinch of salt

SHORTBREAD BASE First make the base. Place all the dry ingredients in a food processor or blender and turn into a powder. Stream in 85ml (⅓ cup) of water with the oil so that the mixture turns into a dough which can roll easily into a ball without crumbling. Once at the right consistency, taste for seasoning. It should be slightly sweet and biscuity.

Press the base mixture into a square tin lined with baking paper and set aside while you make the next components.

HEMP CARAMEL For the caramel, place the soaked dates in a food processor or blender and blend until smooth. Add the Hemp Butter and vanilla, then blend again until everything is well combined and the consistency of caramel. Stream in the oil and keep mixing to help it set. Spread the caramel over the base and put it in the fridge while you make the ganache.

GANACHE Place the chocolate in a heatproof bowl with the oil and Hemp Butter. Bring 200ml (1 scant cup) of water to the boil in a saucepan and when boiling, gradually pour over the chocolate, stirring to combine. This will begin to melt the chocolate, so stir continuously until you have a glossy ganache. Stir through the CBD with the salt to taste. Pour the ganache over the lightly set caramel and leave to set for at least 3–4 hours before serving.

SQUASH AND WALNUT DRIZZLE CAKE

This is a cake for morning, noon and night, and it is packed full of good grains, plants and healthy fats. You can make it into cupcakes or one large cake, as we have done here. They say that baking bread is better than therapy and I would say that baking cake is maybe even better still!

Makes: 1 small loaf

Time taken: 1 hour

80g (3oz) puréed roasted squash, cooled
85g (3oz) olive oil
45g (1½oz) date syrup or honey
60g (2oz) brown rice syrup or agave
60g (2oz) plant-based yoghurt

For the flax egg

1.5 tbsp ground flax seeds
5 tbsp water

For the batter

60g (generous ¼ cup) soft brown sugar
1 tbsp dried sage
80g (3oz) tapioca flour
30g (1oz) oat flour
40g (½oz) buckwheat flour
40g (¼ cup) walnuts, processed into
    a flour
1½ tsp baking powder
¾ tsp bicarbonate of soda (baking soda)
½ tsp salt
1 tbsp ground ginger
100g (3½oz) candied, roasted or
    plain walnuts, crumbled

For the tahini icing

100g (scant ½ cup) tahini
100g (scant ½ cup) oat milk
1 tbsp honey
2 tbsp cacao butter, melted

SQUASH Place the puréed squash in a food processor or blender along with the rest of the wet ingredients. Blend until well mixed.

FLAX EGG Make your flax egg by mixing the ground flax seeds with the water. Leave it to sit for five minutes.

At the same time place the walnuts into the oven on a baking tray and roast them for 12 minutes, until lightly toasted, then remove from the oven and leave to cool.

BATTER Place the remaining dry ingredients in a large bowl and lightly mix together. Fold through the blended wet mixture, making sure that everything is thoroughly combined. Fold through the jelly-like flax egg at the end.

Pour the mixture into 6 cupcake cases or a small lined loaf tin and bake for 35 minutes. Check the sponge is cooked through by inserting a knife in the top and checking that it comes out clean. If it is done, let the cake cool for 5 minutes in the tin and then leave it for another 30–60 minutes out of the tin until it is cool to touch.

TAHINI ICING Meanwhile, make the tahini icing by mixing all of the ingredients together in a large bowl to form a whipped and creamy icing. Transfer to the fridge to firm slightly before icing the top of the cooled cake. Ice the top as we have done here or get as creative as you like. Perfect with a cup of your favourite tea!

TIP – To make the squash purée, preheat the oven to 170°C fan (190°C/375°F/Gas 5). Cut the squash into 2.5cm (1in) cubes and place them on a baking tray. Drizzle with 1 tablespoon of water and 1 tablespoon of olive or coconut oil. Roast for about 30 minutes until soft, then add the squash to a blender or food processor and blend until smooth.

LIFT

THE CHAGA LATTE EXPERIENCE

This recipe started out as a chocolate brownie but I was reluctant to add another brownie recipe to the world, so in the hope of doing things a little bit differently, this cake is laced with shrooms, and has a fermented coffee topping. With the base being squash or sweet potato, they are slightly lower in sugar than regular brownies and extra fibre rich. If you're into coffee flavoured anything you will like this! If not, you can make the base alone and enjoy as a brownie.

Makes: One 20cm square or round tin
Time taken: 8 hours, plus 12 hours fermentation

For the fermented coffee cream base
300g (10½oz) cashews, soaked
2 tbsp live kombucha
150ml freshly brewed coffee

For the walnut brownie base
400g (14oz) sweet potato or winter squash
75ml (⅓ cup) olive oil
80g (generous ½ cup) walnuts, soaked for
    10 minutes and rinsed
15g (1 tbsp) flax seeds
100g (1 cup) chickpea flour
40g (1½oz) carob powder
½ tsp baking powder
¼ tsp bicarbonate of soda (baking soda)
1 tbsp chaga (optional)
2 tbsp coffee grounds (optional)
½ tsp smoked salt flakes
200g (7oz) dark chocolate, finely chopped
80g (⅓ cup) coconut sugar

For the fermented coffee cream flavouring
200g (2 cups) fermented coffee cream
75ml (⅓ cup) oat milk
50ml (scant ¼ cup) strong coffee,
    such as espresso
50ml (scant ¼ cup) maple syrup
120g (1 cup) coconut oil, melted
50g (⅓ cup) cacao butter, melted
1 tsp tamari

For the chocolate glaze
200g (7oz) chocolate, finely chopped
100ml (scant ½ cup) boiling water
3-4 tbsp maple syrup

COFFEE CREAM BASE Blend cashews with coffee until the mixture is thick but smooth. Add the kombucha, making sure the cashews aren't too hot from blending, then blend again until combined. Transfer to a glass bowl, cover and leave in a warm space for 12–24 hours to ferment. The mixture should be aerated and slightly sour smelling when you check it. Once ready, keep it in an airtight container for up to 7 days.

BROWNIE BASE Preheat the oven to 180°C fan (200°C/400°F/Gas 6). Peel and chop the sweet potato into large pieces, then place on a baking tray with 2 tbsp of olive oil and 2 tbsp water. Bake for 30–40 minutes, then leave to cool before blending. Place the walnuts on a baking tray and bake for 10 minutes until they are toasted and crisp, then leave to one side. Whisk the ground flax seeds with 3 tbsp water and let it sit for ten minutes to form a flax egg. Sift together the flour, carob, baking powder, bicarb, medicinal mushrooms and coffee if using, with all but one pinch of the salt in a large bowl. Bring a saucepan of water to boil, then turn the heat down to a simmer. Place 120g of the chocolate in a heatproof bowl with the olive oil and sugar, then gently stir the chocolate until it is melted and the sugar is dissolved. Blend the melted chocolate mix with the sweet potato until you have a smooth mixture. Stir this into the dry ingredients, then chop the walnuts and add them to the mix with the remaining chocolate. Bake at 170°C fan (190°C/375°F/Gas 5) for 15 minutes. Leave to cool completely.

COFFEE CREAM FLAVOURING Blend the fermented cream with the remaining ingredients. This mix should be like a thick creamy latte.

TO ASSEMBLE Choose the shape you want the cake to be. I cut the base into 10 cm (4 inch) circles, but you can also make the whole cake in a cake tin with a spring form base. Pour the fermented coffee cream over the base and leave to set in the fridge for at least 4 hours or overnight.

CHOCOLATE GLAZE When the rest of the cake is set, add the chopped chocolate to a heatproof bowl and pour the boiling water over it. Whisk well to melt each piece of chocolate. Place the set cake or cakes on a cooling rack with baking paper underneath to catch the chocolate. When the glaze is slightly cooled, pour over the cake.

CULTURED LEMON POSSET WITH HOT BLACKCURRANTS

When I was a child, we used to regularly frequent a local restaurant that served this cool and tangy lemon posset with piping hot blackcurrants on top. I was totally mesmerized by the recipe and wanted to create a plant-based version. Fermenting the cashews makes a really big difference in this recipe, as they bring a light tangy flavour that complements the lemon, create a super smooth and utterly luxurious texture and moreover, bring good bacteria into the mix, which makes the cashews more digestible and friendly to the gut.

Makes: 4 pots

Time taken: 20 minutes, plus 6 hours setting time

250g (2 cups) cashew nuts, soaked overnight

1 tbsp kombucha or probiotics

200ml (scant 1 cup) almond milk

Zest and juice of 2 lemons

80g (⅓ cup) honey

1 tbsp nutritional yeast

1 tsp ground turmeric

¼ tsp vanilla extract

Pinch of salt

Pinch of ground black pepper

150g (5½oz) coconut oil, melted

Rosemary Walnuts (see page 153), to serve

For the hot blackcurrants

200g (2 cups) blackcurrants, fresh or frozen

1 tbsp honey

CULTURED LEMON POSSET First, ferment the cashews. Rinse the soaked nuts really well and then blend them in a food processor or blender with 100–200ml (½–1 cup) of water until silky smooth. Once smooth, ensure that the mixture is not too hot. If it's warm, let it cool slightly, then add the kombucha or probiotics and pulse once more to combine. Transfer the mixture to a glass bowl and cover with a cloth. Leave overnight in a warm place to ferment.

The next day, the mixture should be lightly aerated and smell slightly fermented. If your environment is particularly cool, it may take a little longer, or if you are in a hot and humid place, the fermenting time will be significantly quicker.

Blend in the remaining ingredients, except the coconut oil, until very smooth. Stream in the coconut oil while still mixing and blend until everything is well combined. Check that you are happy with the taste and the sweetness is to your liking.

Pour the mixture into ramekins or heatproof glasses and place in the fridge to set for at least 6 hours.

HOT BLACKCURRANTS To make the hot blackcurrants, put the blackcurrants and honey in a small saucepan – if using fresh fruit, add 200ml (scant 1 cup) water to the pan. Simmer the fruit until you have a runny jam consistency.

To serve, take the posset from the fridge and top the cool, set posset with hot berries. Serve with Rosemary Walnuts.

NOTE – It is not essential to ferment these possets, but I highly recommend it. If you don't have time, use cashews that have been soaked in hot water for at least 2 hours and then rinsed. Blend them with the remaining ingredients in place of the fermented cashews by adding 50-80ml (¼-⅓ cup) of extra almond milk.

CHANGE THE MOOD CHOCOLATE POTS

As you may have gathered, desserts for me are always about memories. These little pots are no different and remind me of a shop-bought rich chocolate pot I used to adore. These pots go beyond mere silky chocolate goodness and can be adapted to whatever you need in terms of your mood. If you tune in when you eat this, I'm pretty sure your heart will light up.

Makes: 3 pots

Time taken: 10 minutes, plus 3 hours to set

150g (5½oz) plant-based chocolate, finely chopped

1 tbsp olive oil

1 tbsp mood-balancing mushroom powder of your choice (see caption opposite)

150ml (5fl oz) plant-based milk

¼ tsp salt

Maple syrup, to taste (optional)

Coconut yoghurt, to serve

For the candied cacao nibs

150g (¾ cup) cacao nibs, roasted

2 tbsp maple syrup

Large pinch of salt

For the cherry compote

200g (1 cup) fresh or frozen cherries

1 tbsp maple syrup

TIP – Replace 50ml (scant ¼ cup) of the milk with coffee for a delicious and more energizing result or substitute any of the medicinal mushroom powders for a pipette of CBD for a different result.

Preheat the oven to 150°C fan (170°C/325°F/Gas 3).

CHOCOLATE POTS Place the chocolate in a heatproof bowl with the olive oil and your chosen mushroom powder.

Heat the milk in a saucepan and bring it to the boil, then pour the milk over the chocolate and stir until very well combined. The mixture will become progressively smoother as you continue to stir.

Add salt and taste; depending on your chocolate, you may like to add a teaspoon of maple syrup for sweetness.

Pour the ganache into small glasses or ramekins and leave to set in the fridge for at least 3 hours.

CACAO NIBS To make the candied cacao nibs, combine roasted cacao nibs, maple syrup and salt in a small mixing bowl and spread the mixture out on a baking tray. Bake for 30 minutes until they are roasted and crispy.

Once they are ready, cool them and keep them in an airtight container for up to 1 month.

CHERRY COMPOTE Next, make the cherry compote. If you are using fresh cherries, halve and deseed each one. Place the cherries and maple syrup in a small saucepan over a medium heat and simmer for 10 minutes until they are soft and gooey. Set them aside as you bring everything else together.

Once the ganache is set and cacao nibs are cool, top the ganache with the cherry compote, a spoonful of coconut yoghurt and the candied cacao nibs and enjoy.

MUSHROOM POWDERS	SOOTHE Reishi	FOCUS Lion's mane	BALANCE Chaga	LIFT Cordyceps

PEANUT BUTTER CARAMEL CHEESECAKE

This cheesecake is sweet and salty with a rich raisin biscuit base, sweet caramel, combined with a salty peanut butter cheesecake cream. This cheesecake does take a little patience and I highly recommend following the steps carefully, but rest assured, the end result is totally luscious. You can put everything in the blender and hope for the best, but trust me, you will not get the best result. It will be lumpy and unbalanced. As in life, a little attention to detail with a measure of patience can change everything.

Serves: 6
Time taken: 30 minutes, plus 8 hours setting time

100g (1 cup) pecans
60g (2oz) cacao nibs
100g (1 cup) oats
140g (1 cup) raisins, soaked in hot water
    for 10 minutes and drained
3 tsp coconut oil, melted
1 tbsp molasses
Large pinch of salt
4 tbsp toasted peanuts, crushed, to serve

For the peanut caramel
100g (3½oz) coconut oil, melted
80g (⅓ cup) peanut butter
70g (2¾oz) cacao butter, melted
¼ tsp salt
4 tbsp maple syrup
100ml (scant ½ cup) cool water

For the peanut cheesecake
300ml (1¼ cups) plant-based milk
    (almond works well but oat is also good)
100g (scant ½ cup) peanut butter, unsalted
    (if yours is salted leave out the salt)
1 tsp lion's mane mushroom powder
¼ tsp salt
2 tbsp honey or agave
80g (3oz) cacao butter, melted
50g (1¾oz) coconut oil, melted

"Regardless of whether we consider our
creative talent to be great or small, as long as
it might benefit others it deserves to go
beyond the realm of thought."

—Headspace

Preheat the oven to 180°C fan (200°C/400°C/Gas 6). Spread the pecans and cacao nibs out on a baking tray and bake for 25 minutes until gorgeously roasted. Remove from the oven and set aside to cool.

BASE Pulse the oats in a food processor or blender to form a fine flour. Add the raisins and process again to bind with the oats to form a dough. Once a sticky dough is starting to form, add the melted coconut oil and 3 teaspoons of water into the processor and then continue to blend until a dough is totally formed.

Add the pecans at this point and process the dough once more. The raisin biscuit should easily roll into a ball. If it doesn't, add more oil and water. If you add too much liquid, simply add some more of your blended oat flour to absorb some of the liquid.

Roll all of the dough into a ball and put it between 2 pieces of baking paper. Roll until the entire biscuit base is just 5mm (¼in) thick. Cut with your desired moulds or press into a lined 20cm square tin or a small round tin. Place on a tray in the fridge to set, ready for the next layer.

PEANUT CARAMEL Next, make the peanut caramel. Combine the coconut oil, peanut butter, cacao butter and salt in a food processor or blender and blend on medium speed until well combined.

With the blender running on low, slowly drizzle in the maple syrup and the water and gradually increase the speed as you do so – you should see the caramel become glossy. It may look like it splits and if so, continue to blend until it binds and thickens. If the mixture remains thin, add 2–4 tablespoons more cold water and blend again.

Pour the peanut caramel on top of the biscuit base (or bases) and place in the fridge to set.

PEANUT CHEESECAKE Now, make the peanut cheesecake. Blend the milk, peanut butter, lion's mane powder, salt and honey together in a food processor or blender until smooth. Taste for salt levels, then stream in the melted cacao butter and coconut oil while the mixture is blending – this enables the cheesecake top to set. Pour the mixture over the set caramel and place the cheesecake back into the fridge for at least 3 hours until set.

Place a small frying pan over a medium heat and add the peanuts. Gently shake the peanuts in the pan and toast them until they are golden.

Remove the cheesecake from the mould or moulds, slice it into portions if necessary and serve with the toasted peanuts sprinkled over the top.

TAHINI MOUSSE AND GINGER FLORENTINES

This recipe always surprises those making it as it may look like it will not work until it has had its time setting in the fridge. The joy of this particular dessert is that it is light, fluffy and rich all at once. This can be made with any nuts or seed butters, so have a go at trying different flavours and enjoying the taste and versatility of the mousses you can make.

Makes: 4

Time taken: 8 hours

For the tahini mousse

100g (3½oz) vegan 75% chocolate, chopped

100g (3½oz) coconut oil

60g (¼ cup) light tahini

1 tbsp maple syrup

⅛ tsp salt

For the ginger Florentines

50g (¼ cup) plant-based butter

50g (¼ cup) rapadura sugar
  (or light brown sugar)

1 tsp honey

1 tbsp plant-based cream

1 tsp ground ginger

30 sunflower seeds

2 tbsp black or white sesame seeds

¼ tsp salt

TIP – You could also set the tahini mousse in small glasses or ramekins and serve as they are with a Florentine on the side.

TAHINI MOUSSE Half fill a small saucepan with water and set a heatproof bowl on top. Place over a low heat. Add the chocolate and coconut oil to the bowl and gently stir to melt. Once melted, take the bowl off the heat and set aside for a moment.

Blend the tahini and maple syrup together with 200ml (scant 1 cup) of water in a food processor or blender until smooth. Stream in the melted chocolate and salt and continue to blend. You will have a thin liquid that is sweet and chocolatey. Taste the mixture – depending on your chosen chocolate you may like to add a little more salt or maple syrup to taste. Pour the tahini mousse into a square container to set in the fridge for at least 6 hours, until set to touch.

Preheat the oven to 180°C fan (200°C/400°F/Gas 6). Line a large baking tray with baking paper.

GINGER FLORENTINES Next, make the ginger Florentines. Melt the butter and sugar together in a small saucepan over a medium heat. Once melted, add the honey, the cream and the ginger, bring to the boil and simmer for 3–4 minutes.

Leave the mixture to cool, then stir through the seeds and the salt and roll into 10 small balls. Place them on the lined baking tray with a good amount of space around each one, so they have room to spread.

Bake for 10 minutes until flat and golden. Remove from the oven and leave on the tray to firm up and cool for 30 minutes. Once they are completely cool, transfer the Florentines to a small airtight container until ready to use. They should be crisp and dark bronze in colour.

Boil the kettle and pour the water into a cup. Place a metal tablespoon in the cup to heat. Dry the spoon, take the mousse from the fridge and using the spoon facing you at a 50 degree angle, scoop the mousse into a round shape or a quenelle if you are able to, and place it on a plate. Serve with a Florentine on top.

BLUEBERRY, ROSEMARY AND WALNUT TOFFEE TART

Blueberries are an incredible brain food, not just for their antioxidant properties, but they are also one of the best sources of anthocyanins, which help to reduce inflammation in the brain through fighting free radicals. Of course, they are also here for their taste and there is nothing better than a fresh juicy blueberry, grown in season. Paired with our omega-rich walnuts and memory-supporting rosemary, this blueberry frangipane-filled tart is quite the Mind Food treat.

Serves: 12, makes one 30cm (12in) tart
Time taken: 1 hour

For the pastry
200g (7oz) chickpea flour
200g (7oz) tapioca flour
2 tbsp maca
100g (3½oz) cold plant-based butter or
coconut oil
50g (scant ¼ cup) olive oil
20g (¾oz) rapadura or coconut sugar
1 tbsp chopped rosemary
¼ tsp pink Himalayan salt

For the blueberry jam
200g (1¾ cups) fresh or frozen blueberries
1 tbsp maple syrup

For the walnut frangipane
100ml (scant ½ cup) butter
100g (½ cup) rapadura or organic caster
(superfine) sugar
100ml (scant ½ cup) aquafaba (chickpea water)
250g (2½ cups) walnuts, finely ground
into a flour
3 tbsp buckwheat flour
Zest of 1 lemon
½ tsp baking powder

To serve
Fresh blueberries
Bee pollen

Preheat the oven to 180°C fan (200°C/400°F/Gas 6). Lightly grease a tart tin.

PASTRY Mix the flours with the maca in a large bowl and then add the butter or coconut oil. Lightly rub the flour and butter between your fingertips until it resembles fine breadcrumbs.

Make a well in the middle of the breadcrumbs and add the oil, salt and 1 tablespoon of water. Bring the pastry together with your hands. Add another tablespoon of water as needed and a smooth dough should form. When there are no breadcrumbs left, combine the dough into a large ball, then place it onto a floured surface and roll it out to 4mm (⅛in) thick.

Lightly grease a 30cm (12in) tart tin with a removable base. Carefully place the pastry into the greased tin. It might crack slightly and if so, keep calm and simply fix any cracks with the pastry offcuts. Prick the pastry with a fork a few times to prevent it from rising, and bake in the preheated oven for 5 minutes until lightly golden, then remove from the oven briefly and meanwhile make the fillings.

BLUEBERRY JAM Place the blueberries and maple syrup in a saucepan over a low heat and simmer for 5 minutes until they are slightly caramelized. Set aside.

WALNUT FRANGIPANE To make the walnut frangipane, cream the butter and sugar together in bowl with a whisk. Fold through the aquafaba, walnuts, flour, lemon zest and salt to form a reasonably thick, well combined mixture.

Place half of the blueberries evenly across the base, followed by the walnut frangipane. Bake the filled tart for a further 25 minutes until the pastry is crisp and golden. Remove from the oven and leave it to cool, then cut into slices and top with fresh blueberries and a sprinkle of bee pollen for a wonderful afternoon boost.

PANTRY STAPLES

These pantry staples can be made time and time again to bring your food to life. They all last in the pantry for at least a few months and can be made in large batches so you always have a way to add extra flavour to your meals. A real trick to living the Mind Food life, no matter what you have in the fridge or cupboard, is to add a handful of these condiments to your recipes to take the experience to another level.

Research has shown that crunch literally releases more pleasure in your brain, making us enjoy a meal more, so start with the activated nuts, seeds and granolas. Add some crumbled Rosemary Walnuts (see page 153) to a salad, Brain Dust (see page 153) on top of some hummus and CBD Granola (see page 154) on, well, almost anything! Nut butters are another great trick, especially when they are homemade and they taste absolutely fantastic eaten with fruits, in dressings, drizzled on vegetables or stirred through smoothies. They also make an instant nut milk, just add water!

As we all know, failing to prepare is preparing to fail, so get a head start here and your meals will no doubt be a little more delicious.

SATISFYING SEED ROLLS

These rolls are very simple but effective, they are full of fibre and can be filled with many different flavours. Try filling them with various salads, nut butters, cashew creams or pesto for a totally satisfying lunch.

Makes: 5 rolls
Time taken: 40 minutes

80g buckwheat flour
60g gluten-free oats
90g chia seeds
35g hemp seeds
35g activated sunflower seeds
20g psyllium husk
1 tsp oregano
1 tsp dried rosemary
1 tsp bicarbonate of soda (baking soda)
Large pinch of salt
¼ tsp apple cider vinegar
2 tbsp olive oil
Handful of sprouts like alfalfa or radish
    (optional)
400ml warm water

Preheat the oven to 180°C fan (200°C/400°F/Gas 6). .

Add all of your ingredients to a bowl, pour in the water and mix together with into one big ball. Leave the mixture to rest for 10 minutes.

Grease a medium sized baking tray with a little oil and then roll the mixture into small balls (approximately the size of a tennis ball, or just a bit bigger) and place them onto the baking tray.

Bake the rolls for 30 minutes until golden on the outside. You can test they are done by gently piercing a small knife through one roll; if they are done the knife will come out clean. Once they are cooked through, remove the rolls from the oven and then allow to cool as they will continue baking for a short while after.

Store in a sealed container for up to 3 days. You can serve them cool or heat them up, filled with anything you desire, such as a freshly made hummus (see page 176) and some salad leaves.

BEYOND GREEN CRACKERS

These crackers are packed full of nutrient-dense seaweed, greens and seeds, which are all mineral-rich supporters of a healthy brain. This recipe is great to serve with dips or loaded with salads and vegetables as a raw toast. I especially like to eat it with any of our hummus recipes (see page 176) and loads of sprouts for a great snack or small lunch on the go.

Makes: 1 × 500ml jar
Time taken: 40 minutes

1 tbsp olive oil
1 tbsp white miso
1 tbsp honey
1 tbsp spirulina
Pinch of salt
200g (scant 1½ cups) pumpkin seeds, pulsed into a medium flour
200g (1½ cups) ground flax seeds
100g (¾ cup) hemp seeds
2 sheets of nori seaweed, blended into a powder

Place the wet ingredients in a bowl with 300ml (1¼ cups) of water and stir. Add the seeds and seaweed and stir everything together really well. This should be a medium-wet consistency, with every seed coated in the wet mixture.

Leave the dough to stand for 15 minutes to firm up. At the end of this time the mixture should be much more solid to touch. If it hasn't firmed up then leave it for a little longer until it has.

Carefully spread this mixture onto a piece of baking paper or a silicone baking mat using an offset spatula or a spoon. Try to spread it so that it is about 4mm (¼in) thick. This process in itself is quite meditative – on a rainy day I quite enjoy making big batches of this and spending time just spreading them out.

Once the dough is evenly spread, you can choose to keep the crackers as they are and then snap them into irregular pieces later or score the dough with a metal spatula or the wrong side of a knife, into rectangles or squares.

Either bake in the oven preheated to 100°C fan (120°C/250°F/Gas 1/2) for 20–30 minutes until crisp or dehydrate in a dehydrator for 24 hours at 42°C (107°F) for a wonderfully crisp cracker.

Overleaf, clockwise from top left: Roasted Rosemary and Almond Nut Butter, Hemp Butter, New-Age Nut Butter, Smokernut, Granola Two Ways, Brain Dust, Salad Sprinkles, Spirit Oil, Smoked Nut Butter and Antioxidant Jam.

ACTIVATED SEEDS

Makes: 1 × 250ml jar
Time taken: 15 minutes

125g (scant 1 cup) sunflower seeds
125g (scant 1 cup) pumpkin seeds
1 tbsp olive oil
2 tbsp tamari
½ tbsp dried chilli flakes

Place a frying pan over a medium heat and add the seeds. Toast until they start to cook and pop, then pour over the oil, tamari and chilli flakes. Stir to combine and, once everything is well coated, remove from the heat and leave to cool.

Once cool, transfer these tasty seeds to an airtight jar and keep in the cupboard until you are ready to use.

SALAD SPRINKLES

Makes: 1 × 250ml jar
Time taken: 5 minutes

1 nori sheet, torn into small pieces
200g (1⅔ cups) hemp seeds
1 tbsp chlorella powder
1 tsp garlic powder
½ tsp salt

Place the nori pieces in a food processor or blender and blend into a powdery dust.

Mix all of the ingredients together in a bowl, add the blended nori and mix well. Store in a jar until ready to use.

SPIRIT OIL

Makes: 1 × 1l jar
Time taken: 20 minutes

1 litre (1 quart) olive oil
2 rosemary sprigs
3–4 sage leaves

Toast the rosemary sprigs in a dry frying pan over a medium heat to release the aroma.

Pour the olive oil into a large glass bottle and add the herbs. Leave to infuse for at least 2 weeks before using. Make sure it isn't left anywhere too hot or that changes temperature frequently.

After 2 weeks, use the oil as you wish.

ROSEMARY WALNUTS

These walnuts are a great addition to sweet and savoury dishes, crumbled over porridge, tossed through salad or as a portable snack. Activating walnuts makes a big difference to the taste and crunch, and you won't believe how dark the soaking water becomes, showing there's a lot of stuff on these mighty nuts that you can do without.

Makes: 1 × 250ml jar
Time taken: 1 hour

200g (scant 1½ cups) walnuts, soaked far at least 1 hour, then rinsed well
1 tbsp rosemary leaves, finely chopped
2 tbsp maple syrup
2 tbsp olive oil
½ tbsp lion's mane mushroom powder (optional)
¼ tsp salt

Preheat the oven to 150°C fan (170°C/325°F/Gas 3).

Place the walnuts in a bowl, mix with the other ingredients and set aside while the oven preheats.

Spread the walnuts out on a baking tray and bake for 40 minutes until golden. The long baking time gives a rich and deep roasted result.

Leave the nuts to cool and then place them in a jar or sealed container and store for up to a couple of months.

TIP – Activating means soaking, rinsing and then drying out a nut for optimum nutrition.

BRAIN DUST

This dukkha-style sprinkle is a great way to add flavour to savoury dishes, from a simple bowl of grains and greens to roasted roots or sprinkled on hummus and eaten with crudités.

Makes: 1 × 250ml jar
Time taken: 30 minutes

200g (scant ½ cup) walnuts, soaked far at least 1 hour, then rinsed well
100g (¾ cup) pumpkin seeds, soaked far at least 1 hour, then rinsed well
1 tbsp coriander seeds
1 tbsp cumin seeds
1 tsp dried oregano
1 tsp smoked paprika
1 tsp salt

Preheat the oven to 160°C fan (180°C/350°F/Gas 4).

Spread the walnuts and pumpkin seeds out on a baking tray. Roast for 20 minutes until lightly golden, then leave to cool.

Place a small saucepan over a medium heat and add the coriander and cumin seeds. Toast the spices over a low heat to release the aroma. Remove them from the heat and lightly crush in a pestle and mortar. Do the same with the roasted walnuts and pumpkin seeds.

Season with salt and, once cool, store in a sealed jar for up to a month.

GRANOLA
TWO WAYS

ANTIOXIDANT JAM

These savoury granolas will add an extra crunch to any meal and as mentioned previously, adding a crunch to your food releases more pleasure in your brain. This granola is full of ingredients to boost your day and bring more pleasure to the plate.

Berries are the ultimate brain food, rich in polyphenols and antioxidants. I'm forever finding a way to incorporate at least one serving into each day. This jam (jelly) is filled with berries and a dash of rosemary which adds flavour when poured on porridge, dolloped on top of overnight oats or smothered on pancakes.

Makes: 1 × 500ml jar
Time taken: 30 minutes

Makes: 1 × 250ml jar
Time taken: 40 minutes

WALNUT AND
ROSEMARY GRANOLA

100g (¾ cup) oats
100g (¾ cup) chopped
    walnuts
½ tsp smoked paprika
1 tbsp chopped rosemary
    leaves
50ml (scant ¼ cup) olive oil
20ml (4 tsp) maple syrup
2 tbsp white miso

CBD
GRANOLA

100g (¾ cup) oats
100g (¾ cup) hemp seeds
1 tsp smoked paprika
2 tbsp nutritional yeast
50ml (scant ¼ cup) olive oil
20ml (4 tsp) maple syrup
2 tbsp tamari
1–2 pipettes CBD

500g (5½ cups) frozen berries
    (cherries or mixed summer berries work well)
100g (½ cup) coconut sugar
4 rosemary or thyme sprigs, kept whole

Combine the dry ingredients for your chosen granola in a large bowl. Mix together the remaining wet ingredients in a small bowl until well combined. Pour the wet mixture over the dry and mix thoroughly.

Spread the granola evenly over a piece of baking paper or a silicone baking mat and dehydrate at 41°C (105°F) for between 12–24 hours, or until crispy. Cool before serving or store in an airtight container for up to 2 months.

Place the frozen fruit in a saucepan and pour over the sugar. Leave to sit and thaw for 10 minutes.

Add the herbs and place the saucepan over a medium heat. Simmer the fruit for 30 minutes until the liquid is mostly gone and you have a medium-thick jam-like consistency.

Remove the herb sprigs and discard. Leave to cool completely before spooning the jam into a sterilized jar with a lid. Store in the fridge for up to 1 month.

NOTE – Alternatively, you can bake the granola in an oven preheated to 140°C fan (160°C/325°F/Gas 3) for 10 minutes or until very lightly toasted.

SMOKERNUT

This smoked coconut is very addictive and just wonderful on curries, tossed through salads and in sandwiches. I first discovered this idea when eating a raw BLT sandwich with this coconut 'bacon' and I was hooked. Here's my interpretation, I hope you love it. Be warned: it's addictive!

Makes: 1 jar
Time taken: 30 minutes

100g (1 cup) coconut chips
4 tbsp toasted sesame oil
2 tbsp maple syrup
2 tbsp tamari

2 tbsp smoked paprika
½ tsp smoked salt
2 tbsp smoked water (optional)
½ tsp cumin

Preheat the oven to 150°C fan (170°C/325°F/Gas 3).

Whisk all of the ingredients except the coconut chips together in a medium sized bowl, then add the coconut chips and mix everything thoroughly so that each and every coconut chip is covered in the bright orange marinade.

Leave them to soak up the liquid for 5 minutes, then spread the marinated coconut onto a lined baking tray.

Bake for 20 minutes, until crisp and golden.

Place the tray onto a cooling rack and leave the coconut to cool entirely. Place into a sealed glass jar and store outside of the fridge for up to 2 weeks.

PLANT-BASED BUTTERS

You will see that these nut butters appear in recipes throughout the book and could even be eaten as they are with a spoon. Personally, I love to mix a few tablespoons of my nut butters with a couple of tablespoons of cold water or nut milk to make them into a sauce. This not only makes them last longer but stops that sticky feeling when you eat them out of a jar.

ROASTED ROSEMARY AND ALMOND NUT BUTTER

This is next level almond butter and I hope you will never buy almond butter again after trying this Mind Food version. The taste says it all.

Makes: 300g
Time taken: 1 hour

300g (2½ cups) almonds
2 tbsp olive or almond oil
2 tbsp chopped rosemary leaves
¼ tsp salt

Preheat the oven to 150°C fan (170°C/325°F/Gas 3).

Spread the almonds out on a baking tray and roast them slowly until deep roasted. This will take at least 40 minutes depending on your oven. Leave to cool for 5 minutes so they are warm but not hot.

Transfer the warm roasted almonds (the warmth helps them to blend into a butter) to a food processor or blender along with the oil and rosemary and blend on a high speed. If your food processor is less powerful you may need a little extra olive or almond oil.

Once smooth, add a good pinch or two of salt and pour into a sterilized jar. Make sure the butter is at room temperature before putting on the lid and then storing in the fridge.

HEMP BUTTER

This butter couldn't be easier as it uses just one ingredient – the humble hemp seed. If you don't use hemp already I'm sure these recipes will inspire you to at least give it a try. Enjoy this butter as an ingredient in many Mind Food desserts, or even savoury in Hemp and Sage Hummus (see page 176).

Makes: 300g
Time taken: 5 minutes

300g (2½ cups) hemp seeds, hulled

Blend the hemp seeds in a food processor or blender until a butter forms. This could take 5–10 minutes depending on your machine and you may need to scrape down the sides of the machine every now and then. Just be sure the hemp doesn't get too hot or it will affect the taste.

When you have a smooth hemp butter, leave it to completely cool and then store it in a sterilized jar in the fridge.

SMOKED NUT
BUTTER

This is a slightly different nut butter and does require a special bit of kit, which is a stove-top smoker. There is nothing quite like this butter and it can be used on toast or in cooking just like regular butter. The smoked element is key, but if you don't have a stove-top smoker, you can roast the nuts low and slow and then use smoked salt.

Makes: 1 × 500ml jar
Time taken: 40 minutes plus 6 hours setting

150g (1¼ cups) cashews
100g (¾ cup) pine nuts
30g (¼ cup) melted cacao butter
30g (¼ cup) melted coconut oil
45ml olive oil
60ml (¼ cup) cool water
Zest of 1 lemon, and 50ml lemon juice
2 tbsp nutritional yeast
½ tsp salt

Preheat the oven to 160°C fan (180°C/350°F/Gas 4).

Spread the cashews out on a baking tray and roast them slowly for 20 minutes until golden. Add the pine nuts and roast for a further 5–10 minutes until all the nuts are golden.

Remove from the oven and transfer straight to a food processor or blender with the melted oils and blend until silky smooth. Add the cool water and the mixture will thicken and come together.

Once smooth, add the lemon juice and zest, nutritional yeast and salt. Pour into a sterilized jar or container to cool, then leave in the sealed jar in the fridge to set for at least 6 hours. Keep for up to 2 weeks and use just like any butter for cooking or on toast.

NEW-AGE
NUT BUTTER

This nut butter can be used in so many ways. Spread on toast, drizzled over salads and poured over almost anything! You can also use it as an instant latte by blending 2 tablespoons of the nut butter with a little water and then warming through.

Makes: 1 × 300ml jar
Time taken: 1 hour

300g (generous 2 cups) walnuts
2 tbsp olive oil
½ tsp miso
2 tbsp lion's mane mushroom powder

Preheat the oven to 150°C fan (170°C/325°F/Gas 3).

Spread the walnuts out on a baking tray and roast them until golden and crisp. This could take about 30–45 minutes. Leave to cool until they are warm but not hot.

Transfer the roasted walnuts to a food processor or blender with the oil. If your food processor is less powerful you may need a little more oil. Blend until silky smooth, then add the miso and lion's mane mushroom powder and process until they are mixed through.

Pour the nut butter into a sterilized jar, making sure the butter is at room temperature before putting on the lid and then storing in the fridge.

FAR OUT FERMENTATION

Fermented foods are a key part of Mind Food, not only to add a tang to our colourful plates but because of the benefits for our gut health and minds. The key to these benefits is increasing the biodiversity in our microbiome through eating a wide variety of plants, and eating fermented foods in which a large number of good bacteria are alive and thriving.

The word fermentation comes from the Latin *fervere*, which means 'to bubble' or 'to boil'. Technically fermentation is a form of cold cooking. For those of you who enjoy any sort of laboratory-style cooking, fermentation may just hit the spot. Having these bubbling jars and glowing bottles brewing away in your kitchen is a fascinating process and there is also the benefit of working in huge batches, so that when they are done you will have quick and delicious enhancements to add to your meals indefinitely. Some even make a great snack by themselves. A small bowl of kimchi with leaves, olive oil and seeds is a brilliantly quick and nutritious snack. You can even get creative with the brines from these ferments, making different dressings by mixing kimchi brine with tahini or adding Lacto-chillies (see page 168) to a soup to spice it up.

I hope these ferments give you the confidence to be more playful in your kitchen and amp up the flavours in your food.

CLEVER KIMCHI

Kimchi packs a punch and adds so much to the simplest of dishes with its hot, spicy and utterly unique flavour. If you haven't tried kimchi before, it has a very particular taste that can split the crowd and the smell is also quite potent. If at first it seems a bit too far out to try, ferment for a longer or shorter time and try again until you get the ferment just right for you. The longer you leave the kimchi the softer and more mellow it will become, while a shorter ferment will give more crisp, crunchy and fresh results.

Makes: 1 × 500ml jar
Time taken: 20 minutes, plus 3–5 days ferment

1 large Napa or Chinese leaf cabbage
3 tbsp sea salt
50g carrot, peeled and chopped into
    matchsticks
1 apple, cored
1 fresh red chilli
1 tsp dried chili flakes
2 garlic cloves
2.5cm (1in) piece of fresh ginger
75g (2¾oz) red bell pepper
1 tbsp Gochugaru chilli flakes (optional)

Separate and wash the cabbage leaves thoroughly and tear into small pieces. Sprinkle the salt on the cabbage in a large bowl. Massage firmly with clean hands to release liquid that will form a brine and then add the carrots.

Blend the other ingredients in a food processor or blender into a paste until smooth. Wearing gloves, rub the blended seasoning paste into the cabbage.

Once the cabbage leaves are coated with the paste, and a good amount of water has been released, transfer the mixture, vegetables and brine to a glass container and compress the mixture to ensure all contents are submerged under the brine. This will prevent any spoilage. Make sure the mixture is completely covered with at least 2.5cm (1in) of brine.

Close the lid and leave it to sit somewhere out of direct sunlight and at cool room temperature, ideally 20°C (68°F) for 4–10 days. Check daily and press it down if the cabbage is floating above the liquid. You can use a ceramic fermenting weight to keep the cabbage submerged if necessary.

When the fermentation process is complete, open the jar and remove the weights (if you have used them) and then store in the fridge.

TIP – Use this kimchi in the Qi-beans (see page 87) or with the CBD Stir-Fry (see page 31).

KOMBUCHA

Kombucha is a wonderfully bubbly, flavoursome and delicious drink that is pretty easy to make at home, with incredible benefits for improving gut health as it is full of good bacteria. It is most commonly made with a SCOBY – which is an acronym for 'symbiotic colony of bacteria and yeast' and brewed with tea and sugar. The process of making kombucha involves a little time and care but if you think of your SCOBY like a new pet, something you need to feed and look after, your kombucha will be all the more tasty. You can get your SCOBY online or, if possible, from a fermenting friend. You can even grow your own by pouring a bottle of live kombucha into a glass jar, cover tightly with a cloth and wait for it to grow.

CLASSIC KOMBUCHA

Makes: 1 × 1l jar
Time taken: 10 minutes, plus 6–10 days ferment

4 green or black tea bags (see Tip opposite)
100g (½ cup) sugar
250ml (1 cup) almost boiling water
100ml (1 cup) mature kombucha for starter liquid
1 full-size kombucha SCOBY

FIRST STAGE OF FERMENTATION Place the tea bags, sugar and the nearly boiling water in a mug. Stir to dissolve the sugar and leave the tea to steep for up to 20 minutes. Add a further 500ml (generous 2 cups) filtered colder water to bring the mixture to room temperature. Pour it into a sterilized 1-litre (1-quart) glass container, making sure there is at least 5cm (2in) gap from the top.

Add the mature kombucha, preferably from the same batch you are transferring your SCOBY from. Check the temperature of the tea mixture, making sure it is comfortable to touch. If it is too hot, it can harm the SCOBY and kill the good bacteria. If it feels cool or comfortably warm to touch, add the SCOBY. Cover the jar with a non-porous towel and put an elastic band around the cloth to prevent fruit flies from contaminating the kombucha.

Keep the fermenting kombucha at room temperature, in an environment with a consistent temperature, somewhere where you could be happy to sit for a long period of time (not too hot or cold or in direct light). Leave it to ferment for at least 10 days for the first brew. For a sweeter kombucha, stop the fermentation process after 5 days.

Taste every 2 days, by pouring a little of the liquid into a cup to try, and wait until the kombucha is to your liking.

When ready, pour three-quarters of the golden liquid into a clean glass swing top bottle and seal it.

Repeat the first process with the SCOBY and the remaining kombucha you have just made. For future batches, let the kombucha brew for 3–7 days, depending on your environments (hotter places will ferment everything quicker).

SECOND STAGE OF FERMENTATION This is your opportunity to flavour the batch of kombucha (see the next recipe). At this point always reserve at least 240ml (1 cup) plain kombucha for the starter liquid in your next batch. This is the stage where the brew will become fizzier, so make sure you open the lid and 'burp' the kombucha every day and taste it, by pouring a little into a glass, at the same time to check when it is ready.

TO MAKE KOMBUCHA VINEGAR

To make kombucha vinegar, the aim is to over-ferment the kombucha at the second stage to remove the majority of the sugar from the brew. Make the kombucha as instructed opposite. Leave 1 litre (1 quart) fermented kombucha at the second stage kombucha for an additional week. You can add chillies or rosemary to this ferment for a more aromatic result. Use this vinegar as you would apple cider vinegar and in our Kombucha Chimichurri recipe on page 175.

TO STORE

Store the finished kombucha in the fridge for up to 3 months. While the fermentation will drastically slow down during this time, it will never stop, so be aware that the taste will evolve. You should also open the lid every now and then so the bottle does not explode, just like when 'burping' the bottle in the second stage.

ROSEMARY AND RASPBERRY KOMBUCHA

Makes: 1 × 1l jar
Time taken: 2–4 days

1 litre (1 quart) Kombucha (see opposite)
2 rosemary sprigs
½ tsp coconut sugar
5–6 fresh or dried raspberries

Add all of the ingredients to a swing-top bottle and leave to flavour and fizz for 2–4 days. Each day open the lid to release any excess air and taste a little in a glass to see how it is getting on. When you are happy with the flavour, store the bottle in the fridge and enjoy cold.

TIP – You can confidently use herbal teas instead of green or black teas once your SCOBY has grown enough to pull the layers apart. I recommend getting to grips with the base recipe first and once you have a healthy and happy brewery going on make another brew, in a separate jar, taking 120ml (½ cup) of the live kombucha liquid and adding a cool brew of sweet herbal tea. Chamomile, turmeric and ginger teas all work well, but steer clear of any teas like Earl Grey that have oils or artificial flavours. Happy brewing!

GINGER AND TURMERIC BUGS

Ginger and turmeric bugs are a simple starter culture for making fermented homemade sodas. When adopting a Mind Food lifestyle it is great to include more ginger and turmeric in your day as both help reduce inflammation and increase energy. Ginger roots are rich in yeasts and lactic acid bacteria, making them ideal for fermentation. You can serve these bugs as a morning shot, add a shot to the Pucker-Up Mimosa (see page 116), add a couple of tablespoons to apple juice or top them with sparkling water for a long cool drink on any day.

Makes: 1 × 1l jar
Time taken: 10 minutes, plus 3–5 days ferment

Ingredients needed per day for 4–8 days
4cm (1½in) grated organic ginger root and/or
    turmeric (preferably with skin on)
2 tbsp organic sugar
2 tbsp filtered water

For the secondary fermentation
60ml (¼ cup) of the bubbling bug
    (first ferment)
1 litre (1 quart) sweet liquid, such as fruit juice or
    sweetened herbal tea

BUBBLING BUG Combine the grated ginger or turmeric with the sugar and water in a clean glass jar. Cover with a cloth, several layers of muslin cloth or a coffee filter and leave at room temperature to ferment.

For the next 4–8 days, stir in an additional 2 tablespoons each of grated ginger or turmeric, sugar and filtered water per day.

Your ginger bug is ready when it produces noticeable bubbles, foam, a fizzing sound when stirred and smells yeasty, similar to a beer. Fermentation times vary but this will be after at least 4 days and probably less than 8.

If using a sweetened tea mixture to flavour your ginger bug soda during the secondary fermentation, make sure to cool the tea to room temperature before combining with the ginger bug.

SECONDARY FERMENTATION Combine the bubbling bug and sweet liquid and transfer to swing-top bottles. It is important to use jars specifically designed to hold carbonated beverages, to prevent jars from exploding when pressure builds up.

Leave the mixture to ferment for 1–3 days at room temperature and then transfer to the refrigerator. Fermentation times may vary, so be sure to watch your soda closely to prevent any dangerous explosions resulting from over-fermentation.

Overleaf from left to right: Anti-Inflamatory Kraut, Clever Kimchi, Cultured Pancake Batter (with chickpeas), Rosemary and Raspberry Kombucha, Pickled Broccoli Stems, Classic Kombucha, Lacto-chillies, Cultured Pancake Batter (with buckwheat), Rose Beetroot Pickles and Pink Pickled Onions.

TIP – You can also use this process to make homemade root beer with traditional ingredients such as sarsaparilla, sassafras, wintergreen, juniper, liquorice and dandelion root.

ANTI-INFLAMMATORY KRAUT

Sauerkraut is a German ferment traditionally made with white cabbage and salt. Salting the cabbage draws out the liquid to make its own brine and the ferment thrives through the bacteria living naturally on the cabbage. Use an organic cabbage, as anything sprayed will no longer have this bacteria and will be full of harmful chemicals. This Mind Food recipe varies from the traditional recipe, containing mustard seeds and turmeric, meaning that it can help reduce inflammation while also making it a gorgeous gold colour.

Makes: 1 × 1l jar
Time taken: 20 minutes, plus 3–7 days ferment

1 white cabbage
1–2 tbsp sea salt
1 tbsp black mustard seeds
½ tbsp yellow mustard seeds
½ tbsp ground turmeric
20g (¾oz) turmeric root

CABBAGE Slice the cabbage and discard the wilted, limp outer leaves. Cut the cabbage into quarters and trim out the core. Slice each quarter down its length, making 8 wedges. Slice each wedge crossways into very thin ribbons.

Transfer the cabbage to a big mixing bowl and sprinkle the salt over the top. Begin working the salt into the cabbage by massaging and squeezing the cabbage with clean hands. At first, it might not seem like enough salt, but gradually the cabbage will become watery and limp, more like coleslaw than raw cabbage. This will take about 5–10 minutes. Leave to rest for at least 10 minutes to help release more liquid.

Stir through the remaining ingredients. Transfer handfuls of the cabbage into a swing-top jar and firmly press down to compact the cabbage and release more juice.

Repeat this process until the jar is full, leaving a 2cm (¾in) space for expansion at the top. Pour any remaining brine over the cabbage and make sure the cabbage is completely covered with at least 2.5cm (1in) of brine. You can use a ceramic fermenting weight to keep the cabbage submerged if necessary.

FERMENTATION Close the lid and leave it to sit somewhere out of direct sunlight and at a cool room temperature, ideally 20°C (68°F) for 4–10 days. Check daily and press it down if the cabbage is floating above the liquid. Be aware that fermentation produces carbon dioxide, so the pressure will build up in the jar and needs to be released daily, especially the first few days when fermentation will be most vigorous.

When the fermentation process is complete, open the jar, remove the weights and then transfer to the fridge to chill.

TIP – This anti-inflammatory kraut is a great addition to salads and sandwiches, boosting the good bacteria in your day.

CULTURED CASHEW CREAM

Makes: 1 × 500ml jar
Time taken: 5 minutes,
   plus 12 hour fermentation

250g (2 cups) cashews, soaked for 4 hours and rinsed
100ml (scant ½ cup) filtered water
2 tbsp live kombucha or 1 tsp probiotic powder

Blend the cashews with the water in a food processor or blender until silky smooth, with absolutely no lumps. If this takes a little time and the mixture gets hot, leave it to cool before moving onto the next step.

Blend the smooth cashews once more with the kombucha or probiotic powder and pulse to combine.

Place the mixture in a glass jar or bowl and cover with a cloth tied with a string. Leave somewhere warm overnight to ferment.

The next day, you will see some bubbles appear and the mixture should smell lightly fermented in a good way. If nothing has happened, it may need a little longer until you can see the fermentation process has happened.

PICKLED BROCCOLI STEMS

Makes: 1 × 250ml jar
Time taken: 2 hours

100ml (scant ½ cup) water
50ml (scant ¼ cup) rice vinegar
2 tbsp rapadura or cane sugar
2 tbsp salt
1 tbsp toasted sesame oil
1 broccoli stem (around 100-150g)
2.5cm (1in) piece of fresh ginger

Place the water, vinegar, sugar, salt and sesame oil in a small saucepan and simmer to dissolve the sugar and salt. Turn off the heat and let the mixture cool.

Prepare the broccoli by taking off the woody end and peeling the tough skin from around the edge of the broccoli with a vegetable peeler. Finely cut the broccoli into matchsticks and slice the ginger into strips too. Place the matchsticks into a sterilized jar, then pour over the cooled brine.

Seal the jar and leave to pickle outside of the fridge for a couple of hours, then store in the fridge for up to 1 week.

LACTO-CHILLIES

Makes: 1 × 500ml jar
Time taken: 10 minutes, plus 3-5 days ferment

250ml (1 cup) filtered water
1 tbsp sea salt
250g (9oz) red chillies, washed and roughly chopped
1 garlic clove, peeled

Mix the water and salt together in a jug and stir until the salt dissolves.

Place the chillies and garlic in a 500ml (18fl oz) jar and cover with the salty brine. If the water doesn't all fit, you can use it for something else but there shouldn't be too much left over.

Seal the jar and place on a shelf to ferment, slightly shaking each day for 3-5 days until the chillies are lightly fermented.

Place the chillies and brine in a food processor or blender and blend until reasonably smooth. Store in the fridge.

CULTURED PANCAKE BATTER

Makes: 5 pancakes
Time taken: 5 minutes,
plus 12 hour fermentation

260g (2 cups) buckwheat flour
or chickpea flour
480ml (2 cups) filtered water
Olive or coconut oil, for frying

For flavouring
2 tsp ground nori (as it's a rich
and salty mineral)
1 tbsp charcoal and 1 tsp miso
(for black pancakes)
1 tsp turmeric, salt and
freshly ground black pepper
(for a golden variety)

Blend the flour with the filtered water in a food processor or blender and then transfer to a large bowl. Leave in an ambient place overnight, making sure to cover the container with a cloth to make sure nothing unwanted gets inside.

The next morning, check that there is a light bubble in your batter. If so, it's ready to use. In this time the mixture probably won't over-ferment but if there are no bubbles you may need to leave it for a little longer.

Add your chosen flavours and stir through. Warm a large frying pan over a low heat, add a little olive oil or coconut oil and once hot add one ladleful of pancake batter. Cook for 1 minute on each side until golden. Repeat with the remaining batter.

ROSE BEETROOT PICKLES

Makes: 1 × 250ml jar
Time taken: 10 minutes,
plus 3–5 day pickle

250g (9oz) beetroot, finely
sliced into rounds or peeled
into long strips

1 tsp sea salt
½ tbsp honey
½ tsp rose water
½ tsp pink peppercorn
1250ml apple cider vinegar
150ml (⅔ cup) filtered water

Combine the beetroot with the salt, lightly massaging to soften each and every piece.

Mix together the remaining ingredients in a jug so that everything is well combined.

Pour the brine over the beetroot and pour the mix into a clean and sterilized jar.

Seal the jar and leave at room temperature for 3–5 days, then move to the refrigerator to store for up to 1 month.

PINK PICKLED ONIONS

Makes: 1 × 500ml jar
Time taken: 10 minutes,
plus 1–2 day pickle

3 small red onions, cut into
thin slices
1 ancho chilli, deseeded and
cut into thin slices
180ml (¾ cup) apple cider
vinegar
60ml (¼ cup) olive oil
2 tsp rapadura sugar
½ tsp salt
1 star anise

Place the onions and chilli in a heatproof bowl and set aside.

Heat the vinegar, oil, sugar and salt in a small saucepan over a high heat until boiling. Once it reaches the boil, add the star anise and remove from the heat. Pour the vinegar mixture over the onions and you will quickly see the onions go a psychedelic pink; this colour will improve in the next hours and days.

Leave to cool before storing in an airtight container in the refrigerator. These pink pickled onions are best enjoyed after a few days and will keep for 2 weeks in the fridge.

MAKE A BATCH

Over the years I have learnt time and time again the tricks that help me. These include not leaving too long between meals, not eating too late at night, which is even more crucial if you have any sort of issues with sleep, making sure I am satisfied by my meals and not reaching for snacks and sweeter treats late at night, as this can send your digestion all over the place.

Preparing ahead of time is a wonderful tool for keeping anxiety at bay. Knowing you are prepared for the day ahead and have a plan in place can stop you from overthinking and avoid falling into the trap of becoming overly hungry when your blood sugar drops.

These batch recipes are here to make your week as smooth as possible. They are all simple and delicious additions to any meal and I love to make a big batch of each of these at the beginning of the week, to make life as chilled as possible. Each recipe makes about 5 servings and will last for at least 3 days in the fridge if stored in a sealed container.

Here is an example of what to batch cook in a week:

+ 1 batch of grains
+ 1 batch of massaged kale (see page 178)
+ 1 dip
+ 1 dressing
+ 1 granola
+ 1 yoghurt
+ 2 plant-based milks to be used throughout the week
+ 1 ferment
+ 1–2 sweet dishes

HEMP MILK

Makes: 400ml
Time taken: 10 minutes

100g (¾ cup) hulled
    hemp seeds
300g (1¼ cups) water
1 date, pitted
Pinch of Himalayan pink salt

Place all of the ingredients in a food processor or blender with the water and blend for at least 30 seconds.

Pour the milk into a jar or bottle and keep in the fridge until ready to use. This milk will keep in the fridge for 3 days, so it is best to make small batches little and often.

HEMP YOGHURT

Makes: 400ml
Time taken: 10 minutes

250g (2½ cups)
    hulled hemp seeds
700g (3 cups) water

Blend the ingredients until they are smooth, then simmer in a large saucepan. The mixture split into curds and whey.

Pour the mixture over a nut milk bag or muslin cloth on top of a bowl to collect the curds. .Let the mixture strain outside of the fridge until it has cooled. Place in the fridge for 8 hours with a weight on top of the cloth. The next day, there should be a good amount of whey in the bowl and the curds should look more solid.

To make the yoghurt, whisk the hemp curds in a bowl until they look like whipped cream. You can add a pinch of salt, honey and/or vanilla if you like.

TIP – Any nuts or seeds can be made into plant-based milks, but each one will have a different soaking time. For example, you can make pumpkin or sunflower seed milk by soaking the seeds for 4 hours before rinsing, blending with water and passing through a nut milk bag. Hemp is the only seed that doesn't need soaking or straining.

Nut milks have a longer soaking time, with most nuts best soaked for at least 6 hours, then rinsed, blended, and strained through a nut milk bag. Making your own nut milks is an amazing way to experience new flavours and level up your recipes and nutrients. Try walnut milk in a chocolate milkshake, macadamia milk for the creamiest milk, wonderful poured over granola and strawberries, or Brazil nut milk for a rich and delicious milk best paired with chocolate or made into ice cream!

HOT SAUCE

Makes: 400ml
Time taken: 1 hour

1 roasted red pepper
100g (3½oz) Lacto-chillies (see page 168)
100ml (scant ½ cup) olive oil

Place all of the ingredients in a food processor or blender and blend until smooth.

Pass through a sieve if needed.

Store in the fridge until ready to use.

MACA AND MUSTARD DRESSING

Makes: 200ml
Time taken: 24 hours

100ml (scant ½ cup) olive oil
50ml (scant ¼ cup) apple cider vinegar
1 tbsp Dijon mustard
1 tsp maca powder
½ tsp white miso
½ tsp honey

Place all of the ingredients in a jar and shake to mix.

Store in the fridge and use on salads, grains or bread.

CHILLI CULTURED CREAM

Makes: 500ml
Time taken: 4–6 hours

200g (1⅔ cups) cashews, soaked for 4–6 hours
    and well rinsed
100g (3½oz) Lacto-chillies (see page 168)

Place the cashews and chillies in a food processor or blender and blend until smooth.

Store in the fridge until needed.

KOMBUCHA CHIMICHURRI

Simply mix all of the ingredients together in a bowl and leave to rest for 5 minutes before using.

Store in the fridge in a jar or container for up to 1 week.

Makes: 300ml
Time taken: 10 minutes

30g (⅓ cup) parsley, finely chopped
30g (⅓ cup) coriander, finely chopped
1 shallot, finely diced
2 mint sprigs

1 red chilli, finely chopped
200ml (scant 1 cup) olive oil
100ml (scant ½ cup) kombucha vinegar (see Tip) or ¼ cup apple cider vinegar
1 garlic clove, crushed
Zest of 1 lemon
1 tsp honey
½ tsp sea salt

TIP – Kombucha vinegar can easily be made if you are in the process of making your own kombucha (see page 163). It can be flavoured with herbs, garlic or chilli for an even more flavourful result.

HEMP AND PARSLEY PESTO

Place the hemp seeds and parsley in a food processor or blender and blend to break down the parsley.

Add the remaining ingredients and pulse into a chunky pesto.

Season to taste and enjoy as a dip, on hummus or folded through pasta.

Makes: 500ml
Time taken: 10 minutes

60g (¼ cup) hemp seeds
30g (⅓ cup) parsley, roughly chopped

Zest and juice ½ a lemon
1 garlic clove
100ml (scant ½ cup) olive oil
2 tbsp nutritional yeast
½ tsp chilli flakes
½ tsp salt

MISO MAYO

Add all of the ingredients, except the oil, to a food processor or blender and add 100ml (scant ½ cup) of water. Blend for at least 30 seconds so that everything is silky smooth.

With the blender running slowly, stream in the oil to emulsify. If you don't have a hole in the top of your blender to pour the oil in, just add the oil and blend again.

The result will be a wonderfully creamy, salty sauce, perfect for dipping, drizzling and spreading on many savoury plates. Store the mayo in an airtight container in the refrigerator for up to 5 days.

Makes: 500ml
Time taken: 4 hours

200g (1⅔ cups) cashews, soaked for 4 hours and rinsed
1 tbsp white miso

1 tsp lemon juice, freshly squeezed
1 tsp apple cider vinegar
1 garlic clove
50ml (scant ¼ cup) olive oil

SPROUTED CHICKPEA HUMMUS

Makes: 1 × 500ml jar
Time taken: 40 minutes, plus sprouting time 3–5 days

150g (generous ¾ cup dried chickpeas, sprouted if possible (see page 23)
50ml (scant ¼ cup) aquafaba (chickpea water)
1 tsp white miso
1 garlic clove, roasted
Zest and juice of 1 lemon
½ tsp coriander
½ tsp smoked paprika
¼ tsp smoked salt or 1 tbsp smoked water
100g (2¼ cups) tahini
3 ice cubes

Add the prepared chickpeas to a pot of boiling water and cook for 30 minutes, until soft.

Cool the chickpeas and then add to the blender with the rest of the ingredients, apart from the tahini and ice, adding a little more of the chickpea water if needed, depending on how thick you like your hummus.

Once the hummus is smooth, add the tahini and the ice cubes to make it extra creamy and delicious.

Drizzle with a little olive oil and store in a sealed jar in the fridge. This will keep for up to 1 week.

HEMP AND SAGE HUMMUS

Makes: 1 × 500ml jar
Time taken: 10 minutes

250g (1½ cups) chickpeas, sprouted if possible (see page 23), and cooked
50ml (scant ¼ cup) aquafaba (chickpea water)
100g (3½oz) Hemp Butter (see page 158)
5 fresh sage leaves
Juice of 1 lemon
½ tsp white miso
¼ tsp salt
Olive oil, for drizzling

Place all of the ingredients in a food processor or blender and blend until smooth, adding a little more of the aquafaba if needed, depending on how thick you like your hummus.

Store drizzled with a little olive oil in a sealed jar in the fridge for up to 1 week.

ROASTED CARROT 'HUMMUS'

Makes: 1 × 500ml jar
Time taken: 1 hour

4 large carrots, peeled, washed and cut into 2cm discs
6 tbsp olive oil
1 tbsp paprika
75g (⅓ cup) tahini
1 garlic clove
Zest and juice of 1 lemon
Salt

Preheat the oven to 180°C fan (200°C/400°F/Gas 6). Line a baking tray with baking paper.

Place the carrots on the tray along with the oil, paprika, a pinch of salt and 3 tablespoons of water. Roast for 20 minutes until cooked through and golden. Leave the carrots to cool.

Peel the garlic cloves before blending with the remaining ingredients until smooth.

Place the 'hummus' in a jar and refrigerate before serving.

ROASTED BEETROOT SPLASH

Makes: 1 × 500ml jar
Time taken: 1 hour

2 large beetroot, washed and
    cut into even pieces
2 tbsp oil
35g (¼ cup) walnuts, roasted
Salt

Preheat the oven to 180°C fan (200°C/400°F/Gas 6).

Toss the prepared beetroot onto a baking tray and drizzle with the oil, a pinch of salt and a few tablespoons of water. Roast for 20 minutes until the beetroot is cooked through and soft. Leave to cool.

Transfer the roasted beetroot to a food processor or blender with the remaining ingredients and blend until smooth.

Place in a jar and refrigerate before serving.

TIP – Try making the recipe with Cacao Baked Beetroot (see page 97) instead of the roasted beetroot for a delicious result.

HERB STEM VINAIGRETTE

Makes: 400ml
Time taken: 10 minutes

200ml (generous ¾ cup)
    olive oil
2 large handfuls of mixed herb
    stems (chervil, coriander and
    parsley all work well here)
75ml (⅓ cup) apple
    cider vinegar
1 garlic clove
1 tbsp Dijon mustard
1 tsp honey
½ tsp salt

Place all of the ingredients into a food processor or blender and blend until smooth.

Taste for seasoning and when you are happy, pour the dressing into a glass jar or sealable container. Store in the fridge for up to 5 days.

POMEGRANATE AND CBD DRESSING

Makes: 150ml
Time taken: 5 minutes

2 tbsp white miso
1 tbsp pomegranate molasses
2 tbsp olive or hemp oil
½ tbsp lion's mane
    mushroom powder
1 pipette CBD

Add all of the ingredients to a jar, along with 2 tablespoons of water, and shake to mix.

Store in the fridge and use on salads, grains or on bread.

MASSAGED KALE

Makes: 3–5 portions
Time taken: 10 minutes

500g (1lb 2oz) kale,
washed and dried (you can
also use cavolo nero)

3–4 tbsp olive oil
½ tsp salt

Cut off the bottom ½cm of the kale stalks without cutting off any leaves. Hold that end of the stalk with one hand and with the other, put your thumb and forefinger around the base of the leaves and pull upward slowly, neatly stripping the kale leaves from the stems.

Add the leaves to a large bowl and finely chop the stems before adding them to the leaves and drizzling over the oil and salt. With clean hands, massage the kale. Taste for seasoning and then store your beautifully massaged kale in a sealed container in the fridge for up to 5 days. If you have any leftovers, try the wild green chip recipe below.

WILD GREEN CHIPS

Makes: 1 medium container
Time taken: 30 minutes

1 batch of Massaged Kale
(see above) in any flavour
with nut butter or without

To make great kale chips, the trick is to have your oven at a low temperature or to use a dehydrator. If you are using your oven, preheat it to the lowest setting possible, which is likely to be around 120°C (250°F/Gas 1/2).

Spread the Massaged Kale over a large lined baking tray or two and cook in the oven until crisp. This will take 20–30 minutes depending on your kale and oven.

If you are using a dehydrator, spread the kale out on a dehydrator tray and dehydrate your kale at 50°C (122°F) overnight. Once the kale is totally crisp, allow it to cool and then store in a sealed container and enjoy as a snack or crunchy topping on salads and savoury dishes.

ROASTED ROOTS

Makes: 4–6 portions
Time taken: 50 minutes

2 tbsp olive oil
½ tbsp salt
1 thyme or rosemary sprig

200g (7oz) seasonal root
vegetables, such as carrots,
beetroot, parsnips, squash,
washed, peeled if necessary,
and cut into chunks

Preheat the oven to 170°C fan (190°C/375°F/Gas 5).

Place the prepared vegetables in a large baking tray with the oil, salt, herbs and 2 tablespoons of water. Toss everything together, making sure each piece of vegetable is lightly coated.

Bake for 35–40 minutes, moving the roots around every 10 minutes so that they are cooked on each side, until they are lightly golden and a knife goes through them easily.

Leave the roasted roots to cool completely before putting them into a sealed container in the fridge.

GOLDEN QUINOA

SEASONAL SLAW

Quinoa is a wonderful seed that has become increasingly popular. Used as a gluten-free 'grain', it is a useful ingredient to have pre-cooked and ready to add sustenance to meals. This quinoa is laced with antioxidant-rich turmeric and subtle spices to bring a little extra taste to any day.

This slaw really can flow with the seasons. I have used a nice balance of vegetables here but don't be afraid to switch it up depending on what you have. It's very simple and created to be added into your stir-fries, salads and can even be warmed through and served with grains, leaves and a dressing for a quick lunch.

Makes: 6 portions
Time taken: 10 minutes

200g (generous 1 cup) white, black or multi-coloured quinoa, soaked for a couple of hours and rinsed
1 tbsp turmeric powder
2 tbsp coconut oil

½ tsp dried chilli flakes
¼ tsp smoked salt
⅛ tsp black pepper
Zest of 1 lemon (optional)

Makes: 4–6 portions
Time taken: 10 minutes

1 large carrot, washed and peeled
1 red beetroot, washed and peeled
1 candy cane beetroot, washed and peeled

1 parsnip, washed and peeled
Juice of 1 lemon or orange
2 tbsp olive oil
½ tsp salt

Place a medium saucepan over a medium heat and add 500ml (generous 2 cups) of water. Add the quinoa, put the lid on the pan and bring to the boil. Once boiling, reduce the heat to a simmer and cook for 10 minutes until the quinoa is cooked and the water has mostly evaporated.

Place a piece of kitchen paper between the quinoa pan and the lid and leave it to sit for 10 minutes. This makes the quinoa slightly fluffy and just perfectly cooked.

Remove the lid and paper and add the remaining ingredients and stir to combine. Taste for spice and salt and if you are happy, leave the quinoa to cool completely before placing it in a sealed container in the fridge for up to 4 days.

Grate each of the root vegetables, experimenting with using a box grater for a rustic slaw or a vegetable peeler to make a slaw with ribbons or even a chunky matchstick slaw, if you have good knife skills.

Toss the roots in the oil, citrus juice and salt and leave in the fridge until ready to serve.

This slaw will keep for up to 4 days in a sealed container in the fridge.

THE BEST BROWN RICE

I love having a big batch of brown rice in the fridge to throw into hot or cold meals. This brown rice is lightly seasoned so no matter if you are just topping it with some leaves or throwing a handful into a stir-fry, it will be simple yet delicious. Here, we have the added benefit of the green tea that is infused while cooking; the polyphenols in green tea have been shown to support brain health. Remember, it's all these little things that can make a huge difference.

Makes: 400ml
Time taken: 50 minutes

200g (1 cup) short grain brown rice,
    soaked for a couple of hours and rinsed
1 green tea bag
30g (⅓ cup) chopped parsley
2 tbsp tamari
2 tbsp olive oil

Place a medium saucepan over a medium heat and add 500ml (generous 2 cups) of water and the tea bag. Add the rice, put the lid on the pan and bring to the boil. Once boiling, reduce the heat to a simmer and cook for 35 minutes until the rice is al dente and the water is mostly evaporated.

Place a piece of kitchen paper between the rice pan and the lid and leave the rice for 10 minutes. This makes the rice slightly fluffy and just perfectly cooked.

Place the rice in a large bowl or spread out on a baking tray to cool and then add the parsley, tamari and oil and stir to combine.

Make sure the rice is properly cooled and refrigerated as soon as possible. Then place in a sealed container in the fridge and store for a maximum of 4 days.

When you reheat rice, make sure you do it properly so that the rice is piping hot. Enjoy with many of the Mind Food recipes in this book.

Previous page from left to right: Sprouted Toasted Buckwheat, Roasted Roots, Hot Sauce, Sprouted Chickpea Hummus, Spirit Oil, Maca and Mustard Dressing, The Best Brown Rice, Wild Green Chips, Kombucha Chimichurri, Golden Quinoa, Herb Stem Vinaigrette and Sprouted Toasted Buckwheat.

TIP – Add seaweed to this rice for a more nutrient-packed result. I love to shred a sheet of nori and toss it through the rice or soak some wakame or hjiki and reheat the rice with the oil and seaweed. It makes a perfect lunch on the go with leaves, toasted seeds and a dressing.

SPROUTED TOASTED BUCKWHEAT

This is such a different way to enjoy buckwheat, which really is like no other grain. Buckwheat is in fact a seed so in this recipe we sprout the buckwheat first before toasting it for a nutty accompaniment to any savoury plate. Sprouting the buckwheat is slightly different to sprouting other seeds (see page 23). With buckwheat it is important to soak the seeds for only 1 hour before starting the sprouting process.

Makes: 4–6 portions
Time taken: 40 minutes, plus sprout time
  24 hours

200g (1¼ cups) whole
  unroasted buckwheat
4 tbsp olive oil
2 tbsp tahini
1 tbsp maple syrup
1 tbsp smoked paprika
¼ tsp cayenne pepper
¼ tsp salt

Place the buckwheat in a large bowl or a jar and cover it with plenty of water. Leave the buckwheat soaking for precisely 1 hour and then rinse the buckwheat really well in cold water. The water will most likely be pink and potentially slightly thick.

Place the soaked and well-rinsed buckwheat back into the jar or bowl and cover with a cloth or piece of kitchen paper. Leave the buckwheat to sprout for up to 24 hours until small white sprouts of about 1–2mm (⅛–¼in) have formed. Depending on the environment in your kitchen this could take a little more or less time. Thoroughly rinse the sprouted buckwheat once more and dry it slightly with a piece of kitchen paper or a clean cloth.

Add the rest of the ingredients to a large bowl and mix them well, then toss the buckwheat in the bowl to evenly coat each seed.

Preheat the oven to 170°C fan (190°C/375°F/Gas 5). Leave the buckwheat to marinate while the oven warms.

Spread the buckwheat out on a large baking tray and roast for 20 minutes until lightly cooked but not hard.

Serve hot or leave to cool completely and store the toasted buckwheat in the fridge ready to either reheat or toss through salad in the week.

INDEX

ACKNOWLEDGEMENTS & THANKS

Over the last decade I have had so many incredible people supporting me in the years of suffering, recovering, rediscovering and finally thriving and writing this book. Remembering all the people that have been there through the years has been quite amazing so here it goes....

Firstly, to Juney, my **Mum**, for being the catalyst for me to get better, giving me hope and support then and now. You may not know the power of your positivity and intuition but I certainly do! To my **Dad**, the wise owl, for many words of wisdom and constant support and to you both for always being there to massage kale, step in as commis chefs, trying absolutely anything I make, never doubting that anything is possible and for always bringing pixie dust.

My **grandparents**, those still here and those who aren't, always remind me what strength is and always keep things in perspective. Gardening with my **Gramps** is one of my first memories and that nostalgia often inspires so much of what I do. **Nana** you are my absolute hero and it is such a treat that you are here to see this come to life.

To **Adam** and **Trudy** who gave us all a nudge to face up to what was going on! **Cheryl Edgeller**, who left an eating disorder charity to help me personally, without you I don't know where I would be now, and **Martin John** who found the formula through Chinese herbs and acupuncture that shifted my mindset.

Friends who have encouraged me and stood by me through dark and very light times. Especially **Tiffany**, you were a massive part of this story

and got me through the early days of grief. **Josh**, the only person who truly understood. **Lucy Scott** for many memories, **Connie** for that splinter support, **Libby**, **Hannah**, my spiritual guru **Rebecca** and **Priscilla** for all the podcast dreaming and for reminding me of the power of connection, I'm so grateful to have such lifelong friends.

Those who have drifted away have motivated me even more to share what is possible through lifestyle, being more conscious and more connected has enabled me to understand why they went. It happens when you change and it's the hardest part but the most transformative.

Everyone who has believed in me: **Rob Rees**, for first making me see what *Mind Food* could be in terms of a concept, **Geoffrey Higgins** for opening my eyes to creating a dreamland, **Hilary Chester-Master** and The Organic Farm shop team for making something with such integrity and heart and of course **Kate Lewis**, for creating the Asparaland and allowing me to be part of it and really live my dream, I'm eternally thankful and transformed through the experience.

All the Foodie friends and teachers around the world in Bali, Barcelona, New York, Paris and London, these places have shaped me as a cook and each person that I met along the way taught me so much, not only about flavour and technique but about culture, attitude and endless encouragement. I hold onto this and feel inspired each time I pick up my knife. **Carolina** you had to be in here as you made so much possible and are the best chef I've ever worked with. Every opportunity, especially HOY

Paris, has given me the confidence to do this, **Charlotte**, thanks for your vision and letting me be part of it!

Ayelen, always there to roll truffles, get involved and ready to get stuck into many wild, and sometimes unrealistic, ideas and who helped make many of the desserts for the *Mind Food* shoot!

Gail and **Maddie** who have been a significant part of the Mind Food beginnings and who assisted on the shoot for this book and so many others who have volunteered at events and workshops when I was only just getting started. **Marthe**, **Jasmin**, **Steph** and **Pippa** who were the most thorough recipe testers ever, and all Plant Academy students for supporting and being part of the process.

And of course, to **Monica** for finding me and making *Mind Food* happen, it's been a long time in the making but writing Mind Food over the last part of 2020 and into 2021, marking the ten year anniversary of this journey for me was everything I had ever hoped for. Let's manifest many more chances to work together, it's been a dream! To all the team at Leaping Hare and Quarto, but especially **Charlotte** and **Isabel** for bringing the vision to life and for such enthusiasm throughout!

To my partner in food **Sara** – the book would not be what it is without your images. But thank you also for noticing that we should explore possibilities together and for sharing a vision for food and life that can change the way we all see the world. There are too many words, and hours making those final touches and moving that fork for the millionth time, but since we started working together everything has gone to a whole new level and the way you see, hear and appreciate detail teaches me so much every day!

To all those out there doing the work and paving the way for change, there are so many mental health ambassadors and initiatives that have given me knowledge to share in these pages.

To everyone who finds this book and supports it, you are the ones who can make Mind Food expand and reimagine the world of mental health. Together we can do things differently, believe in the power of plants and talk openly about lifestyle medicine and live the mind food life.

Finally, **Rishi** you were the first one to ever really see me and through all the struggles there was a lot of light, magic and unbelievable sparkle. I'll never get 'over' you and I wouldn't ever want to, that's not what it's about. My first love and real teacher, you are the catalyst to the *Mind Food* magic and I hope this mission prevents even one tragedy like yours. May your light live on in these pages and beyond.

This book is for you, whoever picks it up and takes one step in their mind food journey, you're paving the way for change by being open to possibility.

RESOURCES

MENTAL HEALTH:

CALM
Campaign Against Living Miserably
www.thecalmzone.net
Helpline: 0800 58 58 58

MIND
www.mind.org.uk

HEADS TOGETHER
www.headstogether.org.uk

EATING DISORDERS:

BEAT
www.beateatingdisorders.org.uk

CREDITS

NUTRITION
Anne Marie Berggren RDN, CND, MS, CNSC, FMNP

PRINTED CLOTHES
Sophie Dunster, founder of Gung Ho London and all-around wonder babe! (www.gungholondon.com)

WOODEN-HANDLED KNIVES
Holly Loftus, female knife maker extraordinaire (www.loftusknives.com)

PRODUCE
Shrub Provisions for fresh produce, Hodmedod's beans and pulses, Halen Mon salt and smoked produce, Raw Living adaptogens and tonic herbs

CBD AND HEMP
Good Hemp (www.goodhemp.com)

LOCATION
Our food studio,
The Food Studio in East London

PHOTOGRAPHY
Sara Kiyo Popowa
www.shisodelicious.com

First published in 2022 by Leaping Hare Press,
an imprint of The Quarto Group.
The Old Brewery, 6 Blundell Street
London, N7 9BH,
United Kingdom
T (0)20 7700 6700
www.QuartoKnows.com

Text © 2022 Lauren Lovatt
Photography © 2022 Sara Kiyo Popowa
Design © 2022 Quarto Publishing Group

A catalogue record for this book is available from the British Library.

ISBN 978-07112-6457-1
Ebook ISBN 978-0-7112-6458-8

10 9 8 7 6 5 4 3 2 1

Commissioning Editor: Monica Perdoni
Designer: Michelle Kliem

Printed in China